M000310579

Teaching Success Guide for the Advanced Placement Classroom

Advanced Placement Classroom

Macbeth

Advanced Placement Classroom

Macbeth

Daniel G. Lipowitz and James M. Conley

PRUFROCK PRESS INC.
WACO, TEXAS

Dedication

To our wives:
Lorraine and Michele
For always loving and supporting us and
for allowing *Macbeth* to be part of our daily conversation.

To our children:
Anna and Nathan
Jimmy, Jr. and Joey
You are our joy, our life.

To our parents:
For your constant love and support.

To our siblings and their families:
For your encouragement

Library of Congress Cataloging-in-Publication Data

Lipowitz, Daniel G., 1953-
  Macbeth / Daniel G. Lipowitz and James M. Conley.
     p. cm. -- (Teaching success guide for the advanced placement classroom)
  At head of title: Advanced placement classroom
  Includes bibliographical references.
  ISBN-13: 978-1-59363-375-2 (pbk.)
  ISBN-10: 1-59363-375-0 (pbk.)
  1. Shakespeare, William, 1564-1616. Macbeth--Study and teaching. I. Conley, James M., 1974- II. Title. III. Title:
Advanced placement classroom.
  PR2823.L56 2009
  822.3'3--dc22
                        2009016326

Copyright ©2009 Prufrock Press Inc.

Edited by Lacy Compton
Production Design by Marjorie Parker

ISBN-13: 978-1-59363-375-2
ISBN-10: 1-59363-375-0

The purchase of this book entitles the buyer to reproduce student activity pages for classroom use only. Other use requires written permission of publisher. All rights reserved.

At the time of this book's publication, all facts and figures cited are the most current available; all telephone numbers, addresses, and Web site URLs are accurate and active; all publications, organizations, Web sites, and other resources exist as described in this book; and all have been verified. The authors and Prufrock Press make no warranty or guarantee concerning the information and materials given out by organizations or content found at Web sites, and we are not responsible for any changes that occur after this book's publication. If you find an error or believe that a resource listed here is not as described, please contact Prufrock Press.

•AP and Advanced Placement Program are registered trademarks of the College Entrance Examination Board, which was not involved in the production of, and does not endorse, this book.

Prufrock Press Inc.
P.O. Box 8813
Waco, TX 76714-8813
Phone: (800) 998-2208
Fax: (800) 240-0333
http://www.prufrock.com

Contents

Acknowledgments

With gratitude, we thank the members of the Unionville High School English department. In addition, special thanks go to the Unionville High School faculty, staff, and administration for their tireless effort and pursuit of excellence each day. Particularly helpful were our contributing colleagues: Joseph Ahart, Rob Conti-D'Antonio, Darlene Grilliot, Calvert Hess, Greg Hilden, Kathy Kapp, Fran Mulhern, and Diane Mustin.

We have benefitted from correspondences with Heather Dubrow, Ph.D., the Reverend John Boyd S.J. Chair in Poetic Imagination at Fordham University; and Reverend Michael J. Ryan and Reverend Raymond F. Tribuiani of Holy Martyrs Parish in Oreland, PA.

Preface

Thank you for purchasing *Advanced Placement Classroom: Macbeth*. Our intention is to help you, the educator, find some new and innovative ideas to share with your colleagues and students. More importantly, however, it is our hope that you will discover something new about *Macbeth*. Maybe there is an activity that will aid your students in connecting with a particular character or scene; maybe you, the classroom practitioner, will unearth something interesting that results in a reassessment of your position on a specific point about the play or guides the way you approach your overall pedagogy. Whatever your experience level, whether you are entering your first teaching position or rapidly approaching the days when you can sit and read leisurely without the pressure of having to grade papers, we hope that this text will reawaken a spark for you, or add to a long and lengthy toolkit of classroom activities. Shakespeare gives us opportunities to try new things and delve deeply into the caverns of confusion that lay before us. Embrace this confusion and help your students journey through the complexities that a study of Shakespeare offers.

The activities, notes, and strategies that we present in the following pages, many of which we have incorporated into our curricula over the years, will crystallize your response to the question "Why Shakespeare?" as well as provide a challenging, informative, and creative learning environment in your classroom. The line assignations are commensurate with the Folger Shakespeare Library's *Macbeth* (Mowat & Werstine, 2004).

Our goal is that some of the activities and discussions will bring Shakespeare's words to life for you and your pupils. Long after your students are out of high school, revel in the satisfaction that your unique approach to this play will stay with them and help them tackle other difficult texts.

To the Memory of My Beloved Master, The Author, Mr. William Shakespeare, and What He Hath Left Us

by Ben Jonson

> To draw no envy, Shakespeare, on thy name,
> Am I thus ample to thy book and fame,
> While I confess thy writings to be such,
> As neither man nor muse can praise too much.
> 5   'Tis true, and all men's suffrage. But these ways
> Were not the paths I meant unto thy praise;
> For silliest ignorance on these may light,
> Which, when it sounds at best, but echoes right;
> Or blind affection, which doth ne'er advance
> 10   The truth, but gropes, and urgeth all by chance;
> Or crafty malice might pretend this praise,
> And think to ruin where it seemed to raise.
> These are as some infamous bawd or whore
> Should praise a matron. What could hurt her more?
> 15   But thou art proof against them, and, indeed,
> Above th' ill fortune of them, or the need.
> I therefore will begin. Soul of the age!
> The applause! delight! the wonder of our stage!
> My Shakespeare, rise; I will not lodge thee by
> 20   Chaucer or Spenser, or bid Beaumont lie
> A little further to make thee a room:
> Thou art a monument without a tomb,
> And art alive still while thy book doth live,
> And we have wits to read, and praise to give.
> 25   That I not mix thee so, my brain excuses,
> I mean with great, but disproportioned Muses;
> For, if I thought my judgment were of years,
> I should commit thee surely with thy peers,
> And tell how far thou didst our Lyly outshine,
> 30   Or sporting Kyd, or Marlowe's mighty line.
> And though thou hadst small Latin and less Greek,
> From thence to honour thee I would not seek
> For names, but call forth thund'ring Aeschylus,
> Euripides, and Sophocles to us,
> 35   Pacuvius, Accius, him of Cordova dead,

To life again, to hear thy buskin tread
And shake a stage, or when thy socks were on,
Leave thee alone for the comparison
Of all that insolent Greece or haughty Rome
40   Sent forth, or since did from their ashes come.
Triumph, my Britain; thou hast one to show
To whom all scenes of Europe homage owe.
He was not of an age, but for all time!
And all the Muses still were in their prime
45   When like Apollo he came forth to warm
Our ears, or like a Mercury to charm.
Nature herself was proud of his designs,
And joyed to wear the dressing of his lines,
Which were so richly spun, and woven so fit,
50   As, since, she will vouchsafe no other wit:
The merry Greek, tart Aristophanes,
Neat Terence, witty Plautus now not please,
But antiquated and deserted lie,
As they were not of Nature's family.
55   Yet must I not give Nature all; thy Art,
My gentle Shakespeare, must enjoy a part.
For though the poet's matter Nature be,
His Art doth give the fashion: and that he
Who casts to write a living line must sweat
60   (Such as thine are) and strike the second heat
Upon the Muses' anvil; turn the same,
And himself with it, that he thinks to frame,
Or for the laurel he may gain a scorn;
For a good poet's made as well as born.
65   And such wert thou! Look how the father's face
Lives in his issue; even so the race
Of Shakespeare's mind and manners brightly shines
In his well turnèd and true-filèd lines,
In each of which he seems to shake a lance,
70   As brandished at the eyes of ignorance.
Sweet swan of Avon, What a sight it were
To see thee in our waters yet appear,
And make those flights upon the banks of Thames
That so did take Eliza and our James!
75   But stay; I see thee in the hemisphere
Advanced and made a constellation there!

Shine forth, thou star of poets, and with rage
Or influence chide or cheer the drooping stage,
Which, since thy flight from hence, hath mourned like night,
80   And despairs day, but for thy volume's light.

Why Shakespeare?
"Soul of the Ages"

Why Shakespeare? Ben Jonson refers to him as "Soul of the age!" in the poem reprinted at the beginning of this text (line 17). Perhaps we should amend Jonson's wording slightly to read "Soul of the Ages." William Shakespeare continues to be relevant to every generation; for, like the masters in all fields of art, his creations dramatize universal truths that are not encumbered by time. Jonson lauds Shakespeare's greatness by placing him in the company of the classical Greek tragedians: Aeschylus, Euripides, and Sophocles (lines 33–34). In *Macbeth*, Shakespeare examines the decision-making process of a good man and a hero, one who serves his country in a distinguished way. Why is *Macbeth* relevant? Shakespeare shows us the pitfalls of temptation, a weakness embedded in all human beings. He forces us to empathize with the tragic hero and, like the great Greek dramatists, makes us wonder how we would behave if we were placed in the same set of circumstances.

To act on our dreams without considering the consequences of our actions is not the mark of one who has achieved a level of self-actualization, the understanding of who one is and what one may realistically achieve. Yet, Macbeth and his wife function inside a hallucinatory bubble where they believe that there are few ramifications other than their own rewards. Macbeth hesitates momentarily in his descent, but Lady Macbeth's pressure loosens any moral footing he may still possess.

Why Shakespeare? He helps us to see motifs that we apply to our own lives. The ability to discern peer pressure in its negative guise is a vital skill. The crossroads of free will and fate come into play, as the witches offer Macbeth choices. He soliloquizes, "If chance will have me king, why, chance may / crown me / Without my stir" (I. iii. 157–159). Unfortunately for him and Scotland, he chooses to stir, thereby destroying everything in his way. Clearly, Macbeth and Lady Macbeth have thought about the crown before, but, in this play, the viewer learns that there is a gap between a wish and an action. For Macbeth, his inability to understand that chasm results in a descent into an inescapable abyss.

For your students who are new to Shakespeare, encourage them to reflect on the protagonist's decisions, to compare and contrast the ideas layered in this tragedy. Things do not always appear as they are. Why Shakespeare? He is of his time and of our time, exploring the gray areas that test the human condition that make us who we are, leaving the solid blacks and whites to the lesser dramatists.

Discovering Purpose in Teaching the Bard

From the most inexperienced middle school/high school student to the Advanced Placement and college-level student, one of the first things that students say when asked about Shakespeare's plays is "Shakespeare's language is too hard to understand." What can they not understand about tales that are filled with treachery, deceit, sex, murder, supernatural beings, and a plethora of dirty jokes? As educators, we sometimes find ourselves "selling" an author or a work of literature to a reluctant audience; it just goes with the territory of being a high school teacher. After a while, however, many students will come around to the side of enlightenment (a marriage of good pedagogy and the student's increased interest level). Yet, Shakespeare in the 21st century still puzzles students, long after we have disseminated, enacted, quizzed, researched, and written about various aspects of his plays in class. Why does this enigma, Shakespearean text, still haunt the classroom walls that we inhabit each day?

Assessing Student Readiness for Shakespeare

As you begin to read and apply this study guide to your teaching and illumination of *Macbeth*, we would like you to examine your response to the question that each educator has had to consider: "Why Shakespeare?" Your answer to this question may be very different from the responses of your pupils. Take a moment to ponder your own teaching practice at the beginning of each unit of study:

- How do you assess your students' readiness to tackle a new topic in literature?
- What prior knowledge and schema exist in their knowledge banks about Shakespeare writings?
- How can you, "the sage on the stage," bring his writing to life?

- How do their responses focus your teaching practice?
- What critical reading approaches contribute to clarifying the text?

Recently, we surveyed a group of our 12th-grade students prior to beginning an intensive study of *Hamlet* and *Othello* at varied academic preparation levels. With a high degree of consistency, a majority of our students responded that Shakespeare was dull because his writing did not relate to today, his language was too hard to understand, his plays are confusing, and reading his plays in class is pointless. Although our students reflect a small sample of high school students, what can we learn from their responses? These are daunting propositions prior to beginning any unit of study, regardless of the subject matter or discipline, yet these challenges define our true nature as educators. Many of us entered the teaching profession to enlighten these very students searching for meaning and connections in literature.

Often students are reluctant to criticize Shakespeare beyond the previously two stated comments of "too hard" and "confusing" because they do not know how to interpret and interact with Shakespeare's plays, and many of us (the teachers in the room) treat Shakespeare as the celebrity of English teachers worldwide. Don't believe us—just take a look around your classroom or at your workspace. Most likely, there is a poster depicting his image and numerous titles of his plays crowding your bookshelves. Shakespearean iconography in English classrooms is the "nerdier" equivalent to the velvet Elvises or the poker-playing dogs; his image is everywhere. OK, so maybe we are embellishing this point a bit, but his artistry envelops our lives. There are many among us who look toward our Shakespearean unit(s) with enthusiasm, trepidation, or more than likely, a combination of the two.

The growing excitement stems from the suggestion that Shakespeare and his writings are seminal to the human experience. Like most of the literature, drama, and poetry that we include in our curricula, Shakespearean drama transcends time and place; Shakespeare's assessment of human behavior remains accurate. Scholars would agree that this observation is not merely rhetorical hyperbole of an English teacher. Issues that his characters struggle with across the canonical works of Shakespeare directly relate to the human experience, particularly with adolescents. These issues include:

- coping with the death of a parent/loved one;
- being in love, most likely for the first time;
- feeling uncertain about self-identity;
- feeling lost in the world;
- having to make choices and painfully comprehending that not every choice has a positive outcome;

❧ coming to the realization that the world is far different from the one presented at a young age; and

    ❧ recognizing that there are people in the world who are selfish and do not care about how their actions affect others.

Although Shakespearean text provides students with remarkable examples of inspired writing, educators often are very reluctant or ill equipped to be critical of the Bard's words. However, be mindful that students will take their cues on literary analysis from their teachers; not allowing them the room to criticize may stunt their love of Shakespeare's poetry and glimpses into the human heart. As scholars, while we may be able to disagree with an interpretation of a specific character, we should all strive to make the unclear, clear, and help students to see the value in Shakespeare. Critical analysis will promote a deeper understanding through higher order thinking and interpretation.

Prior to beginning *Macbeth*, the age-old expression, "the teachable moment," must be considered. Make your mark on your students during these moments; teachers certainly are unaware when they may appear and for how long they will persist. Revel in these times; they are the unplanned instances when the classroom dynamics sustain and energize us.

Underpinnings: Critical Approaches to *Macbeth*

Although there are numerous schools of literary criticism ranging from the traditional historicist/new historicist approaches of textual analysis to the new criticism and postmodernism movements of recent literary research, we feel very strongly that our approach in *Advanced Placement Classroom: Macbeth* will provide many historical connections that, when presented, will help to extrapolate a thorough understanding of the play in the Advanced Placement, honors, or academic classroom. The new historicist approach asks the reader and classroom practitioner to examine the social, economic, and political underpinnings that constitute the structure of a work of literature; our study of *Macbeth* falls under this category of literary critique. Shakespeare was a man of his times who skillfully crafted his dramas accordingly. Therefore, his overt and sometimes concealed feelings are embedded in his texts, disguised in allusions and themes that may be unclear to the 21st-century reader. We would argue, and some scholars may disagree with us, that literature has the history of its artistic expression embedded within the words of its composition. The contemporary references by Shakespeare in his works, some that may be either unknown to the reader and/or beyond the scope of a close-textual analysis of a specific play, are important in the artistic landscape of the play. Lilian Winstanley's *Macbeth, King Lear, and Contemporary History* (1970) clearly echoed these sentiments:

> Shakespeare did not write for the men of the twentieth century nor for men of the nineteenth century; he wrote for the men of the sixteenth and early seventeenth centuries and thus the interpretation that the men of his own day would be likely to place upon his plays is exceedingly important. (p. 1)

There may be Shakespearean scholars who choose to examine his works from a contradictory critical slant. This teaching guide to *Macbeth* attempts to establish that the play is filled with numerous references to contemporary and social events, of which Jacobean audiences would have been aware, regardless of their varied educational background and social strata.

Jacobean England, specifically during the first performances of the *Macbeth* in 1606, was a time rife with suspicious activities that threatened King James I with assassination, specifically, the Gunpowder Plot of 1605. As a result, a great many productions were heavily censored, and playwrights were "forbidden to represent contemporary monarchs upon the stage even if they [the monarchs] were represented in a favorable light" (Winstanley, 1970, p. 4). Because Elizabethans and Jacobeans were prohibited from discussing these ideas in a public forum, theatergoers attended performances with the foreknowledge that the stage played a significant function by remaining in close proximity to the events of the day. Concealing their personal feelings toward political events, playwrights utilized a high degree of symbolism and often shrouded their words in distant historical characters and events so that audience members could connect their contemporary times to those of past generations.

In attempting to expound on historical events throughout this guide, we anticipate that classroom practitioners will be able to connect the contemporary issues of the early 17th century to their effective close-textual reading in the 21st century. We have detailed a number of significant historical events that Shakespeare incorporated into his productions, not only to provide a "theatrical tweaking" to the hierarchy and society of his time, but also to examine the human psychology of the individual character.

Finally, the classroom practitioner must be aware of the presence of King James I in the audience for the inaugural production of *Macbeth*. Specifically, its subject and themes are closely connected to the Scottish ancestry of James, a topic of great interest to the new monarch of England. Shakespeare and other playwrights of the 17th century would have written laboriously not only to avoid the severe censorship of the time, but also to impress their new king.

Shakespearean Language Barriers

Working with students with a wide range of backgrounds has afforded practitioners the opportunity to generate lessons and activities for diverse learning styles. It is incumbent upon the Shakespearean educator to have a sense of comfort with the Bard's language, as well as to model a level of flexibility when teaching Shakespeare. Educators should be mindful that the syntax in Shakespeare, particularly for students who may be encountering his writing for the first time, can be an obstacle that inhibits their initial engagement to the play.

Think of the first time that you read Shakespeare. How were you able to understand the Bard? You probably had an inspiring English teacher who was able to unlock the mysterious blank verse and language that frequently traps the first-time reader. In every generation great people in history have read a number of Shakespeare's plays. Yet, Shakespeare's language is for all ages, not merely reserved for the higher levels of schooling in most secondary and postsecondary institutions. With that being said, allow your students to read and listen to the language and play with and interact with his words, even if you or your students feel silly performing Shakespeare's works.

Shakespearean language transforms our classrooms into a cold castle in Denmark, the Scottish highlands, or the streets of Verona, and provides an escape from our ordinary worlds into magical realms where moral and upstanding citizenry interact with evil and vile creatures. Consequently, we have dedicated Chapter 2 to close-textual reading of and brief activities or discussion points for the play and Chapter 8 to more lengthy activities reserved for enacting and interacting with the play in your classroom—enjoy them!

Macbeth:
A Literary and
Analytical Look

Along with *Hamlet, Othello, King Lear*, and *Romeo and Juliet*, Shakespeare's *Macbeth* stands as one of the most widely studied and teachable plays in Shakespeare's canon of tragedies. The play is a staple of high school literature because it is filled with numerous motifs that the Shakespearean novice, like the groundlings of the Bard's time, can appreciate: blind ambition, blood, murder, and sleep (or lack thereof)—a concept probably more pertinent than any other issue in the adolescent perspective.

This chapter will provide a close-textual reading of each scene and comment on the characters, key events, and Shakespearean motifs. In addition, assignments that are relevant to the scene and the whole play are included for educators regardless of teaching experience. The line assignations are commensurate with the Folger Shakespeare Library's *Macbeth* (Mowat & Werstine, 2004).

Act I: Macbeth's Heroics
and the Temptation of Power

Scene 1: Fair Is Foul and Foul Is Fair

The curtain opens with the three witches or Weïrd Sisters. Originating from Anglo-Saxon, the term *wyrd* means fate or destiny. Throughout the play the witches, who are other worldly beings, conspire to tempt Macbeth to make the wrong choices. The witches resolve to meet Macbeth on his return from battle "upon the heath" (I. i. 7). An essential phrase in the opening scene is "Fair is foul, and foul is fair"

(I. i. 12). This phrase establishes two key comments about the witches. On one hand, they are hypocritical, on the other, they should not be trusted.

The witches speak in *trochaic tetrameter*—a stressed syllable followed by an unstressed syllable. This speech pattern is slightly different from the other characters in the play.

Scene 2: Meet and Greet the Warrior or Is it Warrior-King?

Macbeth's heroic exploits against the "Norweyans" are extolled by a wounded sergeant (referenced as Captain). Macbeth's bravery and ferocious victory over the rebel leader, Macdonwald, is described graphically when the sergeant tells King Duncan that Macbeth "unseamed him from the nave to th' chops, / And fixed his head upon our battlements" (I. ii. 24–25). In addition, Ross informs King Duncan that the captured Thane of Cawdor betrayed Scotland by assisting Sweno, the King of Norway. King Duncan sends Ross to "Go, pronounce his present / death, / And with his former title greet Macbeth" (I. ii. 74–76). The former thane will be executed, and Macbeth will take over his title. A thane is, in essence, a landowner, given property by the king. Before the play begins Macbeth already is the Thane of Glamis.

ACTIVITY: SIMILES AND METAPHORS

Have students identify the similes and metaphors in this scene and explain their meaning. Also, get the students in the habit of citing the line location of each answer. Ask students to read their examples aloud, including the lines where the text appears.

Scene 3: Witches on the Heath

Note how the second witch says that she was "killing swine" in line 2, indicating a curse she placed on someone. The first witch chats about how a sailor's wife rudely refused to share chestnuts with her and sent her away, so the witch set about transforming herself into a rat (without a tail), to seek vengeance against the sailor (Muir, 1992). Witches were known to possess the ability to control winds. To make money, they would sell them to naïve sailors (see I. iii. 12). In order to make their charms effective, legend states that they required body parts. This necessity would explain their proximity to the battlefield.

"Peace, the charm's wound up" (I. iii. 38) indicates that the link between the witches and Macbeth has been set in motion. The metrical structure called *prosody* is reflected in Macbeth's first line: "So foul and fair a day I have not seen" (I. iii.

39). Because Macbeth's language is so similar to that of the witches, Shakespeare foreshadows a connection between them.

ACTIVITY: ONE-PARAGRAPH RESPONSE

Evaluate the different responses of Macbeth and Banquo to the witches' greeting. Why would the witches' greeting startle Macbeth, but not Banquo? Consider the possibilities.

Banquo observes that Macbeth is startled by the witches' hail of Glamis, Cawdor, and "king hereafter" (I. iii. 53). Banquo, in a manner resembling someone questioning a fortuneteller at a county fair, asks the witches to look into the future for him. The witches, for example, predict that he will be the father to a line of kings, but will not be one himself.

Ross and Angus, as instructed by King Duncan, report the news to Macbeth that he is officially the Thane of Cawdor. The series of asides that follow indicate how Macbeth begins to take the witches' remarks seriously. Macbeth reveals to the audience that, perhaps, he was thinking about being king, just thinking, without any desire to act on his traitorous thoughts: "Two truths are told / As happy prologues to the swelling act / Of the imperial theme" (I. iii. 140–142). The truths are that Macbeth, once Thane of Glamis, now is Thane of Cawdor.

Perhaps, more importantly, Macbeth says, "If chance will have me king, why, chance may / crown me / Without my stir" (I. iii. 157–159). As the plot unfolds, Macbeth forgets this particular thought and does, indeed, "stir," setting into motion his reign as king.

ACTIVITY: ONE-PARAGRAPH RESPONSE

Review Banquo's speech to Macbeth (I. iii. 134–138), beginning with "'tis strange." What is revealed about Banquo's and Macbeth's character from this speech? Contrast the two characters.

Scene 4: Duncan Greets the "Unseaming" Macbeth and Banquo

The scene opens with King Duncan asking about the execution of the traitorous Thane of Cawdor. Shakespeare structures the dialogue between Duncan and his son Malcolm so that Macbeth, the future traitor, ironically enters immediately after Duncan says, "There's no art / To find the mind's construction in the face. / He was a gentleman on whom I built / An absolute trust" (I. iv. 13–16).

The crown of Scotland in this time period was not hereditary; therefore, "a successor was declared in the lifetime of a king. The title of Prince of Cumberland was bestowed upon the heir as the mark of his designation" (Muir, 1992, p. 25). Duncan appoints his oldest son, Malcolm, as the Prince of Cumberland. (For further study on the topic of tanistry, see Chapter 4.)

Macbeth's desire to become king begins to surface with the aside. He says, "Stars, hide your fires; / Let not light see my black and deep desires" (I. iv. 57–58). Angrily, Macbeth asserts, in an aside, that Malcolm is now an obstacle that he must "o'erleap, / For in my way it lies" (I. iv. 56–57). Now two must die, Duncan and Malcolm, for Macbeth to achieve his goal. His apostrophe, "Stars, hide your fires," (I. iv. 57) may foreshadow his plan to assassinate Duncan during the night. An *apostrophe* is a figure of speech wherein a character directs his words to an imaginary person or an abstract idea as though the item or person were in the character's presence.

Scene 5: Lady Macbeth Needs a Hobby or Don't Talk to Spirits

In discussing this scene, note that Macbeth has been fighting a war on behalf of Scotland; therefore, he has been away from his wife for months. He sends her a letter detailing his meeting with the witches. You will observe that the witches' "Thou shalt get kings" (I. iii. 70) prediction for Banquo is conveniently bowdlerized from Macbeth's message, leaving Lady Macbeth to believe that her husband met the witches alone.

ACTIVITY: EXPLICATE THE LETTER TO LADY MACBETH

Consider the details presented to Lady Macbeth in her husband's letter. Is Macbeth honest in his reporting? What do you observe about Lady Macbeth's reaction in the opening lines of scene 5?

In her soliloquy Lady Macbeth worries that Macbeth's kind nature will deter him from doing what is necessary to be king. Curiously, she mentions Glamis and Cawdor, but has difficulty vocalizing the ultimate goal—king—replacing the word with "What thou art promised" (I. v. 16). Lady Macbeth reinforces the Anglo-Saxon interpretation of wyrd with her reference to the Weïrd Sisters in these lines: "fate and metaphysical aid doth seem / To have thee crowned withal" (I. v. 32–33). Lady Macbeth, certainly acting as ambitiously as her husband, is conceiving a plan based on incomplete information.

ACTIVITY: BEYOND THESE WALLS

Research current and/or historical events assessing a leader's decision. Evaluate the ramifications of his or her decision. Consider the influence of the social attitudes of the times in which the decision was rendered, or, like Lady Macbeth, whether or not the decision was based on false or incomplete data.

Throughout the soliloquy Lady Macbeth is continuously thinking, "My husband will be king, my husband will be king." Observe her response to the messenger's line "The King comes here tonight" (I. v. 35). Because her thoughts have been consumed by her husband's potential ascent to the throne, she says, "Thou 'rt mad to say it" (I. v. 36).

Furthermore, Lady Macbeth calls on evil spirits to "unsex me here" (I. v. 48). Her intention is to remove her femininity and to act without regret. The Jacobean period audience would have literally interpreted Lady Macbeth's call to spirits as an invitation for evil to transform her (Rowse, 1963). She also indicates that she will carry the knife herself (I. v. 59). Of particular note is Lady Macbeth's greeting to Macbeth—"Great Glamis, worthy Cawdor, / Greater than both by the all-hail hereafter!" (I. v. 62–63). Her remarks echo the witches' greeting of Macbeth on the heath (see I. iii. 53).

HISTORICAL NOTATION: LIVY'S *HISTORY*

According to Holland's translation of Livy (Godshalk, 1965), the Roman historian, Lady Macbeth's character may have been the direct result of Shakespeare's reading of Livy's *History*, a common text in grade schools during the 16th century. Her character may be based on Tullia a woman who, "plotting with her sister's husband, Tarquin, had her husband and sister murdered after which she marries Tarquin" (Godshalk, 1965, pp. 240–241).

Tullia urges her husband to kill her father, Servius the king. Livy suggests that insanity is the price Tullia pays for her crimes. Godshalk (1965) indicates "parallels between Lady Macbeth and Tullia: ambition, incitement to murder the reigning monarch and subsequent insanity" (p. 241).

In this scene Lady Macbeth introduces the appearance/reality motif as she excitedly anticipates Duncan's demise. Observing her husband's honest face, she worries aloud whether or not he can be read "as a book where men / May read strange matters" (I. v. 73–74).

Historical Notation: Hospitality Customs

Dating back to ancient times, hospitality customs were cultural trusts placed on all citizens due to the vulnerability of travelers in global communities. Clearly, these "strangers in a strange land" might not have been aware of the customs of the local community that they would have encountered. With a goal of helping foreign travelers feel at home, customs were developed to limit potential threats of violence to outsiders. On a more global scale these customs, however, were more than an attempt to limit hostilities. Rather, these traditions were akin to the modern idea of "paying it forward." They were revered by nomadic cultures worldwide because they represented a lifeline for all travelers when they would leave their homes and venture into other regions.

In the Bible there is a great deal of emphasis placed on the role and responsibility of the host to provide food, water, and shelter to the guest of the house. By accepting the traveler, the host held the sacred duty of protecting his guest from all harm; clearly, this expectation is one of the codes that Macbeth and Lady Macbeth violate when Duncan is murdered under their roof.

Scene 6: Duncan's Day Trip to the Macbeths

Duncan and Banquo report that Inverness, Macbeth's castle, looks and smells pleasant. Banquo observes that even birds set up their nests here. Greeted by Lady Macbeth, King Duncan thanks her for the trouble he causes, noting his entourage. Practically speaking, a king's visit involves feeding and housing the royal family, their attendants, guards, and servants. Visitor and hostess exchange pleasantries as Duncan enters the castle.

Scene 7: Leaving the Table Before Dessert Is Served: How Rude!

Opening with a soliloquy, this scene immediately reveals the agitation Macbeth is feeling. Assassinating Duncan is occupying all of Macbeth's thoughts to such an extent that he must step away from the welcoming banquet to ruminate. But his thoughts comprise only the consequences of the murder in this speech, not the morality of the act.

The soliloquy begins with Macbeth unwilling to face the consequences of the murder in this life; he will worry about his soul in the afterlife. He says, "We'd jump the life to come" (I. vii. 7). He determines that being "his kinsman and his subject [argue] / Strong both against the deed" (I. vii. 13–14). Macbeth also observes that Duncan is his guest and, "as his host, / Who should against his murderer shut the door, / Not bear the knife" (I. vii. 14–16). In addition, Macbeth considers Duncan's ability to govern and exercise power and determines that his kind persona further argues against taking action. Only Macbeth's "Vaulting ambition" justifies the traitorous act (I. vii. 27). With that reason in mind, Macbeth concludes that ambition alone is an insufficient reason to proceed.

The Force of Lady Macbeth's Persuasion

Lady Macbeth interrupts Macbeth's train of thought, and he declares that he is halting the murder plot. He weighs the options and he deduces, rationally, that based on the above determinants, they should proceed no further. He indicates that he does not want to diminish the many honors bestowed upon him because of his heroism: "Golden opinions from all sorts of people, / Which would be worn now in their newest gloss, / Not cast aside so soon" (I. vii. 36–38).

Lady Macbeth's response indicates that attaining the crown was discussed between them previously. "What beast was 't, / then, / That made you break this enterprise to me?" (I. vii. 53–55). Leading into the above quotation is Lady Macbeth's retort to her husband's change of mind: "Art thou afeard / To be the same in thine own act and valor / As thou art in desire?" (I. vii. 43–45). She references the adage about the cat that would eat fish, but not get its feet wet in Act I, scene vii, lines 48–49. This maxim is a challenge to the manliness of Macbeth. To question Macbeth's virility is to question his being. After all, Macbeth is the warrior who "unseamed [Macdonwald] from the nave to th' chops, / And fixed his head upon our battlements" (I. ii. 24–25). Duncan rewarded his bravery with the additional title of Thane of Cawdor. Lady Macbeth's retort of "What beast was 't" reinforces Macbeth's cowardice. A man of action would never go back on an oath. To indicate the seriousness of her husband's retraction, Lady Macbeth sets up a comparison that shocks the modern audience, certainly. She would smash a breastfeeding baby "had I so sworn as you / Have done to this" (I. vii. 66–67). Samuel Taylor Coleridge views Lady Macbeth's harsh response as not being indifferent, but actually demonstrating a cognizance of no tie greater than the infant being fed by the mother (Muir, 1992).

Lady Macbeth's Plan

While Duncan is sleeping, Lady Macbeth plans to drug the chamber servants so that they will pass out. Then the unguarded Duncan will be easy to kill. Macbeth is convinced by his wife and suggests that the sleeping guards be marked with their own daggers. Lady Macbeth says the plan is credible because they will "make our griefs and clamor roar / Upon his death" (I. vii. 90–91).

The act concludes with Macbeth reinforcing the appearance/reality motif of "fairest show" disguising what "the false heart doth know" (I. vii. 94, 95–96).

> ## ACTIVITY: CHARACTERIZATION
>
> Compose a profile of either Macbeth or Lady Macbeth. Citing lines from the text, review the circumstances that prompt their remarks to each other, in soliloquy and to others.

Act II: Duncan's Death:
Nothing but "Vaulting Ambition"

Scene 1: Macbeth Takes a Stab at Ad-Libbing

Banquo in the first few lines says that the meeting with the witches perturbs him. He comments to his son, Fleance, that he is tired and is having difficulty sleeping. "A heavy summons lies like lead upon me, / And yet I would not sleep" (II. i. 8–9). His thoughts preoccupied with the witches, Banquo reveals the "cursèd thoughts," the witches' predictions, that occupy his mind (II. i. 10). Banquo, like any loyal citizen, would be troubled by any dream involving the witches. Olive Henneberger (1946) concludes in her essay entitled "Banquo, Loyal Subject" that Banquo does not have any designs on the throne. Macbeth then enters the scene. Banquo says he "dreamt last night of the three Weïrd Sisters. / To you [Macbeth] they have shown some truth" (II. i. 25–26). Macbeth lies and says, "I think not of / them" (II. i. 27–28). Of course, Macbeth has not stopped thinking about the witches. He also asks Banquo to meet sometime to discuss the encounter both of them experienced.

Macbeth quietly asks Banquo for his political support in the future. Banquo says that he will "keep / My bosom franchised and allegiance clear" (II. i. 37–38). Possibly Banquo considers Macbeth's request to mean that they will talk about future alliances when they speak later. Either way, Banquo subtly reveals that he supports the king.

After Banquo leaves, Macbeth hallucinates and sees a dagger. Note that he poses a question immediately. Later he asks if the dagger is "sensible / To feeling as to sight? Or art thou but / A dagger of the mind, a false creation / Proceeding from a heat-oppressèd brain?" (II. i. 48–51). Macbeth thinks that the floating dagger is not only just a figment of his imagination, but also an object as tangible as the one he clutches in his hand. The floating dagger leads him to Duncan's bedchamber. Note Macbeth's reference to "Hecate's off'rings" (II. i. 64) and "Tarquin's ravishing strides" (II. i. 67). Hecate is associated with witchcraft from ancient

Greek mythology. Tarquin is the Roman King from Shakespeare's poem *The Rape of Lucrece,* who, with evil intention, moves toward his victim.

Scene 2: Duncan Meets His Doom and Macbeth Murders Sleep

Lady Macbeth reviews the plan for the audience—drunken, snoring servants (grooms), drugged drinks, and daggers easily placed for Macbeth's use. Most importantly, Lady Macbeth confesses that Duncan's resemblance to her father precludes her direct participation in the murder; perhaps she is not as amoral as she had hoped (see Chapter 4 regarding Lady Macbeth's connection to the historical Gruoch and Duncan). In addition, Lady Macbeth notes that she "heard the owl scream and the crickets cry" (II. ii. 20). The owl and the cricket are associated with predicting death (Muir, 1992).

ACTIVITY: CHARACTER ANALYSIS

Compare Lady Macbeth's soliloquy (I. v. 45–61) to her remarks about her father (II. ii. 16–17). What do you conclude about Lady Macbeth's character? Cite specific lines for support. Why doesn't she kill Duncan?

After the murder Macbeth instantly regrets his action. Lady Macbeth reports that Malcolm and Donalbain were "lodged together" (II. ii. 36). After Macbeth heard "God bless us" (II. ii. 37), he notes that he "could not say 'Amen'" (II. ii. 39).

ACTIVITY: SMALL-GROUP DISCUSSION

Why would Macbeth see a dagger? What is Shakespeare telling the reader/audience about Macbeth's state of mind? Also, if you were the play director, how would you stage this scene? Would you show the audience a dagger or not? Justify your answer.

To comfort her husband, Lady Macbeth says, "These deeds must not be thought / After these ways; so, it will make us mad" (II. ii. 45–46). Reflecting an emotional decline, this remark foreshadows the demise of the Macbeths.

In another hallucination Macbeth discloses that he heard a voice cry, "Sleep no more! / Macbeth does murder sleep" (II. ii. 47–48), and then "Glamis hath murdered sleep, and therefore / Cawdor / Shall sleep no more. Macbeth shall sleep no more" (II. ii. 55–57).

ACTIVITY: RESEARCH PAPER

Research the importance of sleep for human beings. Consider the emotional, physiological, and intellectual effects of sleep deprivation. Create a chart that traces behavioral patterns over time when one cannot sleep. Predict how the Macbeths will act over the course of the play if they are sleep-deprived.

Macbeth carries the daggers out of the room in violation of the plan devised by Lady Macbeth (II. ii. 62–64). Lady Macbeth takes the bloody daggers and returns them to Duncan's chamber to smear his blood on the sleeping guards, a difficult task, perhaps, considering that she just compared Duncan to her father. Or, perhaps her action is a practical response to the situation. She does say, "The sleeping and the dead / Are but as pictures. 'Tis the eye of childhood / That fears a painted devil" (II. ii. 69–71).

To intensify the scene further, knocking occurs at the castle door. Macbeth exclaims that he needs "great Neptune's ocean [to] wash this blood / Clean from my hand" (II. ii. 78–79). Ever practical, Lady Macbeth admonishes her husband's hyperbole, calmly advising him that "A little water clears us of this deed" (II. ii. 86). In addition, she reminds Macbeth that, to avoid suspicion, they must change into their nightgown or sleeping clothes. The classroom practitioner may want to note the biblical allusion to Pontius Pilate when Lady Macbeth references the washing of hands to rid them of the stain of Duncan's blood: "When Pilate saw that he could prevail nothing, but that rather a tumult was made, he took water, and washed his hands before the multitude, saying, I am innocent of the blood of this just person: see ye to it. Then answered all the people, and said, His blood be on us, and on our children" (Matthew 27:24–25).

"Wake Duncan with thy knocking. I would thou / couldst" (II. ii. 94–95), the closing lines of the scene, offers segue into the porter scene.

Scene 3: Who's a-Knock, Knock, Knockin' at the Gate?

The traditional academic interpretation of the porter scene is one of comic relief. After witnessing the brutal murder of a king, the Jacobean audience concludes, according to the general thinking among English teachers, that Shakespeare has offset the violence with a lighter touch. The scene features a drunk, half-asleep knave who makes historical references, speaks with sexual innuendo, and just wants to go back to bed after being out late "carousing till the second / cock" (II. iii. 24–25).

Imagining himself as the gatekeeper of a "hell gate" (II. iii. 2), the Porter believes he would be very busy letting in souls. In "Macbeth and His Porter," Tromly (1975) asserted that the Porter is a microcosm of Macbeth, not a contrasting comic figure. He wrote that when the Porter compares Macbeth's castle to hell, his comments are truer than he realizes. Each "imaginary sinner" he admits is a composite of Macbeth (Tromly, 1975, p. 152). The figures are a farmer who hangs himself because he overestimated the market price and hoarded crops; an equivocator, based on the Gunpowder Plot's accused Father Garnet, who commits treason; and an English tailor who steals cloth that belongs to another. (See Chapter 5 for further discussion on the Gunpowder Plot and Father Garnet).

ACTIVITY: RESEARCH ESSAY

Research and generate an essay about the Gunpowder Plot. Consider its causes, the key conspirators behind the plot, its effect on James I's treatment of Catholics, and/or formulate a hypothesis on the reason for its reference in the porter scene.

The Porter's entrance gives the Macbeths time to wash off Duncan's blood and to change their clothes. Tromly (1975) wrote that the three imaginary sinners reveal segments of Macbeth's crime and his inevitable punishment. With the farmer the audience sees that "private gain has triumphed over the public interest" (Harcourt, 1961, p. 394). Macbeth, by killing a king, is the ultimate traitor. By becoming king Macbeth wears a crown and clothes that do not fit (Harcourt, 1961). The tailor reference is reinforced through clothes imagery, as will be seen in later scenes.

The Porter opens the door and admits Macduff and Lennox with the anticipation of receiving a tip: "I pray you, remember the porter" (II. iii. 21). These words, however, are more than a supplication for money. Rather they are an ellipsis, "I pray you, remember the porter['s words]," that foreshadows the discovery of the murdered Duncan, signaling the end of Macbeth's heroism.

Macduff and the Porter banter about the relationship between excessive drinking and its effect on lechery. The dramatic irony occurs when the porter's small sins are contrasted with the enormity of the treachery that occurred in Inverness. Every reference in the Porter's lines has one meaning for him and another for the audience (Harcourt, 1961). Consider "Who's there, in th' / other devil's name?" (II. iii. 7–8). The Porter mentions Beelzebub earlier in the speech. Does the audience make the association to Lady Macbeth?

ACTIVITY: CLASS DISCUSSION

To whom is the porter referring when he says "in th' / other devil's name?" (II. iii. 7–8). Evaluate the options and justify your response.

Macduff observes that Macbeth is awake and explains that the king ordered Macduff to meet with him very early. "I'll make so bold to call, / For 'tis my limited service" (II. iii. 57–58). After Macbeth leads Macduff to the door of Duncan's chamber, Lennox describes the storm of last night. Because the Jacobeans believed that the king was God's representative on Earth, any unnatural death (Duncan's murder) would be manifested through the physical world. Lennox details: "chimneys were blown down, [. . .] / Lamentings heard i' th' air, strange screams of / death, [. . .] the earth / Was feverous and did shake" (II. iii. 62–69). Macbeth's response, "'Twas a rough night" (II. iii. 70), comes across as a textbook example of understatement.

Reacting to the News of Duncan's Murder

Reinforcing the Elizabethan/Jacobean view of the king's deity, Macduff says, "Most sacrilegious murder hath broke ope / The Lord's anointed temple" (II. iii. 77–78). Macbeth and Lennox exit to Duncan's chamber, as Lady Macbeth enters into the courtyard wondering aloud about the cacophony. Macduff cries out, "O horror, horror, horror!" (II. iii. 73) and later, "Murder and treason!" (II. iii. 86). Lady Macbeth, in response to the news, says, "What! In our house?" (II. iii. 103). Banquo reproves her with "Too cruel anywhere" (II. iii. 104).

ACTIVITY: SMALL-GROUP DISCUSSION

Does Lady Macbeth's reaction to Duncan's death constitute a mistake in judgment? Or is it a normal, but inept response to a horrible situation? Review Banquo's remark, too (II. iii. 104).

In a speech blatantly filled with hypocrisy, Macbeth says, "Had I but died an hour before this chance, / I had lived a blessèd time" (II. iii. 107–108). Although he plays the part of loyal citizen, he perhaps does not realize the ironic truth behind his words. At this moment Scotland honors Macbeth as a hero for his bravery against Macdonwald. Of course, this view is about to change. As King Duncan's sons, Malcolm and Donalbain, enter the scene, Macduff informs them of their father's murder. Lennox affirms suspicion on Duncan's guards because of the daggers and the blood. However, Macbeth shifts the murder plan by confessing to killing the guards in Act II, scene iii, lines 124–125. Macduff immediately responds, "Wherefore did you so?" (II. iii. 126).

Macduff's reply indicates shock and anger, and, as the reader will eventually realize, suspicion. What Macduff recognizes immediately is that Duncan's guards would never act of their own accord. The guards' station in Elizabethan/Jacobean society is too insignificant to kill someone of royalty, a king no less. Even if they had performed the heinous act, someone would have bribed them.

Macbeth explains that his love for Duncan overtakes his logic and, thinking about Duncan's murderers just lying there, he had to act, an act of love for his king.

ACTIVITY: BEYOND THESE WALLS

Research the assassinations of John F. Kennedy or Dr. Martin Luther King, Jr., and their alleged assassins, Lee Harvey Oswald and James Earl Ray, respectively. Consider the evidence and determine whether these men acted of their own accord or killed on behalf of others.

Whether in an act of emotional agitation or a calculated response to Macbeth's actions, Lady Macbeth faints. During this time Malcolm and Donalbain, in an aside, comment on the contrasting reactions to their father's murder. They are quiet, while those around them are outwardly distraught. "Let's away. Our tears are not yet brewed" (II. iii. 145), Donalbain says.

At the same time Banquo pledges to find the murderer. "In the great hand of God I stand, and thence / Against the undivulged pretense I fight / Of treasonous malice" (II. iii. 152–154). Macduff concurs. According to Muir (1992), Banquo may be referring to Macbeth's interest in killing Malcolm.

Malcolm and Donalbain decide that there are enemies all around them. "Where we are, / There's daggers in men's smiles. The near in blood, / The nearer bloody" (II. iii. 164–166). Donalbain will escape to Ireland and Malcolm will go stealthily to England. Unlike their father they do not trust the appearances of the supposed friends that surround them.

ACTIVITY: CRITICAL READING EXERCISE

A key motif of *Macbeth* is appearance/reality. Go through Acts I and II and cite lines that reinforce this motif. Consider how theses lines reflect character temperament.

Scene 4: How About This Weather We're Having?

Ross and the Old Man function as a Greek chorus, commenting on the events that have transpired since Duncan's murder. The Old Man notes that he has witnessed unusual events in his 70 years, but "this sore / night / Hath trifled former knowings" (II. iv. 3–5). Ross and the Old Man exchange observations: an eclipse, a falcon attacked by an owl, and Duncan's highbred horses becoming cannibalistic.

Macduff enters and, when asked, comments reluctantly on the evidence. He says that the guards appear to be the murderers, but he concludes, "They were suborned" (II. iv. 35). As noted earlier, Macduff does not believe that the guards acted independently, observing that Malcolm's and Donalbain's fleeing makes the two sons appear guilty. Ross says that the crown will likely pass to Macbeth. Macduff reports that Macbeth has traveled to Scone to be crowned, while Duncan's body will be interred at Colmekill, where Scottish kings are buried.

Macduff Votes With His Feet

"Will you to Scone?" asks Ross. "No, cousin, I'll to Fife," Macduff replies (II. iv. 49–50). This simple exchange deepens Macduff's character and identifies him as a person of high moral standing. His discomfort with Macbeth's decision to kill the guards before they were questioned and the quickness with which Macbeth is crowned forces Macduff to take a stand. By choosing to return to his castle at Fife and not attend the coronation, Macduff publicly declares his opposition to King Macbeth, a decision that infuriates Macbeth. (See Chapter 4 for a textual analysis of Raphael Holinshed's *Chronicles of England, Scotland, and Ireland* [Hosley, 1968] and Macduff's decision). Ross says he will attend the ceremony. The Old Man ends the act with a blessing that prays for better times and echoes the "fair is foul, and foul is fair" remark uttered initially by the witches in Act I, scene i, line 12 and paraphrased later by Macbeth in Act I, scene iii, line 39.

Act III: Accusations and More Murder

Scene 1: Oh, Great! An Invitation to the Macbeths

In addition to the citizens discussed in the previous scene, Act III opens with Banquo, who, with Macbeth, heard what the witches predicted directly. Like the Old Man, Macduff, and Ross, Banquo questions the legitimacy of Macbeth's rule, and, most importantly, concludes that Macbeth, "As the Weïrd Women promised [. . .], / played'st most foully for 't" (III. i. 2–3). Said in a soliloquy, Banquo's words analyze the past events and wonder whether the witches' predictions will be equally as favorable for him. Macbeth enters with Lady Macbeth and repeatedly reminds Banquo not to forget the feast that evening. He also asks him about his riding and if his son, Fleance, will be joining him.

Being summoned to the Macbeths for a feast is not a welcomed invitation in Scotland. The last honored guest, Duncan, did not live long after the dessert was served.

Moreover, Macbeth ironically enflames the hoped-for rumor about Malcolm and Donalbain not only being the murderers, but also "filling their hearers / With strange invention" (III. i. 35–36).

Observe how Macbeth references himself in the plural, the royal "we." For example, "We hear our bloody cousins are bestowed" (III. i. 33) or "To make society / The sweeter welcome, we will keep ourself / Till suppertime alone" (III. i. 45–47).

"To Be Thus Is Nothing" Soliloquy

Macbeth has determined that Banquo is a threat to him. He exclaims that possessing the crown is not enough if he cannot reign without fear of a daunting enemy. "To be thus is nothing, / But to be safely thus. Our fears in Banquo / Stick deep [...] (III. i. 52–54). Knowing how well Banquo has fought, Macbeth recognizes, whether correctly or not, that he is a worthy opponent. In addition, as the reader of the play realizes, Banquo is the only other person to have personally experienced the encounter with the witches. Macbeth sees him as a personal threat. "There is none but he / Whose being I do fear;" (III. i. 59–60). Macbeth proceeds to justify the reasons for Banquo's demise: He "chid the sisters" (III. i. 62) when they called Macbeth king; "they placed a fruitless crown / And put a barren scepter in [Macbeth's] grip;" (III. i. 66–67), but blessed Banquo's sons, his descendents, as kings. With the murder of Duncan, Macbeth worries that he put his soul in jeopardy, "mine eternal jewel" (III. i. 73), so that Banquo's progeny may rule.

ACTIVITY: SOLILOQUY ANALYSIS

Analyze the "To be thus" soliloquy. Why would Macbeth perceive Banquo as a threat? Explicate the lines in the soliloquy carefully. Consider other scenes to supplement your answer.

Two murderers enter. Macbeth notes that the three of them have met previously and Macbeth has spoken to them about Banquo's poor treatment of them. Generally, the two hired assassins are portrayed as poor men, not professional killers. Macbeth's arguments indicate that the men need some persuasive examples, in addition to money, to act against Banquo. Landowners, such as Banquo, Macbeth implies, have treated these men poorly, "held you / So under fortune" (III. i. 84–85), by dispossessing them of their property. Continuing, Macbeth says that this time one should not, as the Bible says, be "so gospeled / To pray for this good man and for his issue" (III. i. 98–99). Macbeth explains that he is giving these men a chance to right the wrongs committed against them and to suffer the insults from these abusive landowners no longer. He reinforces that this fact is the reason for their second meeting. Appealing ironically to their manliness, Macbeth offers a litany of dog species, noting their similarity to each, but reinforcing their differences.

The murderers, desperate men, acknowledge that the world has treated them poorly and each would welcome an opportunity to set things right. The First Murderer responds, "So weary with disasters, tugged with fortune, / That I would set my life on any chance, / To mend it or be rid on 't" (III. i. 126–128). After confirming that Banquo is truly all of their enemies, Macbeth tells the murderers his reasons for hiring them. Recognizing the political consequences of openly killing Banquo, Macbeth acknowledges that, although he has the power to order Banquo's death, he must not, because they share mutual friends: "And though I could / With barefaced power sweep him from my sight / And bid my will avouch it, yet I must not, / For certain friends that are both his and mine, / Whose loves I may not drop" (III. i. 134–138).

The murderers concur as they await Macbeth's command. Macbeth says that he will "Acquaint [them] with the perfect spy o' th' time" (III. i. 149). According to Muir (1992), Shakespeare may have meant "spial," as in observation spot instead of "spy"; otherwise, why would Macbeth wait until later to introduce another murderer? To complete his plan, Macbeth orders the murderers to kill Fleance, too.

ACTIVITY: ONE-PARAGRAPH RESPONSE

Why would Macbeth order Fleance's death, too? What possible benefit would he gain from killing Banquo's only son? Cite textual evidence to support your answer.

Scene 2: Counting Sheep Because I Cannot Sleep

From the initial meeting with the witches through the plan to murder Duncan to Macbeth's coronation, Lady Macbeth and her husband have had little joy. Lady Macbeth attempts to comfort her husband: "What's done is done" (III. ii. 14). However, the consequences of their actions reverberate in the nightmares each has nightly. Their despair and depression are expressed by Macbeth when he exclaims: "Better be with the dead, / Whom we, to gain our peace, have sent to peace, / Than on the torture of the mind to lie / In restless ecstasy" (III. ii. 22–25).

Macbeth admires Duncan for his ability to be finished with "life's fitful fever" (III. ii. 26) and to sleep well. In this scene Shakespeare extends the sleep motif. Lady Macbeth reminds him about the importance of being cheerful for the evening banquet they are hosting. Macbeth responds with another established motif—appearance/reality: "unsafe the while that we / Must lave our honors in these flattering streams / And make our faces vizards to our hearts, / Disguising what they are" (III. ii. 36–39).

Macbeth is astute in his observation that he and his wife are not safe if they must continue to pretend to be something they are not.

Macbeth's plan to kill Banquo occurs without his wife's involvement. She asks, "What's to be done?" (III. ii. 50). He answers, "Be innocent of the knowledge, dearest chuck, / Till though applaud the deed" (III. ii. 51–52). Macbeth then calls out to "seeling night" (III. ii. 52). Personifying night, Macbeth compares it to a falcon whose eyelids are sewn, so that "night's black agents to their preys do / rouse" (III. ii. 59–60). Macbeth wants night to hide the evil he plans against Banquo. In the text, note how the line leads with "Good things of day begin to droop and drowse" (III. ii. 58). This line reinforces the appearance/reality motif. Macbeth's plan: Let the evil work continue under the cover of darkness.

Scene 3: The Murder of Banquo: "I Want What I Want When I Want"

Maintaining the tone of his rule, Macbeth sends a third murderer to join the two whom he hired. The First Murderer challenges the new person, but the Second Murderer accepts the Third Murderer as a necessary addition to reinforce the task they are expected to complete.

ACTIVITY: ONE-PARAGRAPH RESPONSE

What can you deduce about Macbeth's character when he sends a third murderer, "the perfect spy o' th' time" (III. i. 149), to join the other two assassins? What does Macbeth's action reveal about his leadership?

The murderers ambush Banquo and Fleance, but, in keeping with the witches' predictions, Fleance escapes. Scene iii is brief, but its significance is important in understanding Macbeth's persona. At this juncture in the plot, what a reader or viewer may predict is an inevitable, though delayed, confrontation between a vengeful Fleance and an older Macbeth.

First, Macbeth justifies the murder of Banquo as a way to counter the witches' hailing [Banquo] "father to a line of kings" (III. i. 65). Macbeth accepts the witches' remarks about his being Thane and then king, but tries to counter the prediction that favors Banquo. Rather than just accept the witches' remarks completely, Macbeth is determined to pick and choose the predictions that favor him. Banquo told Macbeth earlier in the play to be wary of the "instruments of darkness" (I. iii. 136). Second, Fleance is too young to seek revenge against Macbeth. Shakespeare dismisses Fleance as an insignificant presence in the play.

Scene 4: Guess Who's Coming to Dinner?

The banquet scene opens with Macbeth telling the guests to sit around the table according to their status. As Lady Macbeth welcomes the company, the murderer appears at the door to give Macbeth a report about Banquo. Macbeth, of course, is pleased to hear the news about Banquo, but indicates that Fleance's escape ruins his sense of security: "But now I am cabined, cribbed, confined, bound in / To saucy doubts and fears" (III. iv. 26–27).

ACTIVITY: LANGUAGE SEARCH

See Act III, scene iv, line 26. Locate other examples of alliteration in *Macbeth*. How does Shakespeare employ this literary device to ameliorate meaning or develop character? Find examples of alliteration in daily advertisements (commercial and/or political). Why would a company or political campaign use alliteration? Analyze your examples.

Also, Macbeth, although initially unnerved by Fleance's escape, recovers and dismisses Fleance as a threat for now: "The worm that's fled / Hath nature that in time will venom breed, / No teeth for th' present" (III. iv. 32–34). The murderer is dismissed with a promise that they will talk again. Lady Macbeth chastises Macbeth for so discourteously ignoring the guests at the party: "To feed were best at home" (III. iv. 39), that is, a banquet is more than just eating. That task can be accomplished at home. A host must continually entertain his guests, welcoming them and reassuring them of the joy the host feels among their company. While Lady Macbeth comments on the behavioral expectations of a host, the reader or viewer is reminded of the abhorrence of Duncan's murder by the one who is most responsible for shielding his guest from any harm.

ACTIVITY: POWERPOINT PRESENTATION

Select a country and research the customs and mores of host-guest behavior. What rituals are involved? Is there a specific greeting or a traditional expectation of a type of food or drink?

Banquo's ghost appears, continuing the cycle of hallucinations Macbeth experiences. Unlike the floating dagger or the apparitions seen in the company of the witches, Macbeth has a breakdown in front of his guests. To reassure the nobles, Lady Macbeth steps in by pretending that her husband has had these fits since childhood. "My lord is often thus / And hath been from his youth. Pray you, keep seat" (III. iv. 64–65).

Calling her husband aside, she tries to calm him and to take control of an unraveling situation. Lady Macbeth asks him if he is a man and then reminds Macbeth and the audience about the dagger: "This is the air-drawn dagger which you said / Led you to Duncan" (III. iv. 75–76). Each example, she says, "would well become / A woman's story at a winter's fire, / Authorized by her grandam" (III. iv. 77–79). Macbeth continues to see Banquo's ghost. Finally, Lady Macbeth reminds Macbeth that her guests are feeling awkward and he becomes rational momentarily. Macbeth explains his "strange infirmity" (III. iv. 104), begins to make a toast, sees the ghost, and loses his nerve again. After the ghost departs, Macbeth regains his composure.

Lady Macbeth says, "You have displaced the mirth, broke the good / meeting / With most admired disorder" (III. iv. 132–134). Lady Macbeth's reaction works on both a literal and symbolic level. Firstly, Macbeth's outburst certainly has ruined the feast. Secondly, Shakespeare's word choice reminds the reader or viewer of the larger theme: The Macbeths' murderous actions continue to cause disorder. Scotland is in disarray and Lady Macbeth's response functions as a microcosm of the consequence of the Macbeths' ambitious attainment of the crown.

The guests are summarily dismissed. Alone, Macbeth analyzes his current situation, citing references that speak to Banquo's murder and the discovery of the murderer (Muir, 1992): "It will have blood, they say; blood will have blood. / Stones have been known to move, and trees to / speak" (III. iv. 151–153). According to Muir, stones mark the location of the murder victim, which could be the opening clue in determining the murderer. The "trees speaking" is an allusion to Virgil's *Aeneid*, where a ghost speaks from a tree (Muir, 1992).

The conversation shifts to Macduff, who, by consciously choosing not to attend Macbeth's coronation at Scone, publicly declared himself opposed to Macbeth's crowning. Macbeth is watching Macduff, noting that he keeps "a servant fee'd" (III. iv. 164). In other words, Macbeth has a spy working in Macduff's castle.

ACTIVITY: MOTIFS

Reread the play and locate lines that explain the motifs of appearance/reality, sleep, night, and/or blood. Cite the lines and describe the context in which each line is delivered.

Macbeth says, "I will tomorrow / (And betimes I will) to the Weïrd Sisters" (III. iv. 164–165). Macbeth is determined to seek out the witches. In the first part of the quotation, according to Muir (1992), Shakespeare may have intended a reference to Macbeth sending for Macduff. He interrupts himself and shifts his attention to the witches: "All causes shall give way" (III. iv. 168). Seeing the witches, as Macbeth asserts, is his first priority. He then reveals that he is "in blood / Stepped in so far" (III. iv. 168–169) that there is an equal sign between stopping the killing or continuing the mayhem. Either decision will result in the same outcome for Macbeth. His speech concludes with a reference to decisions that must be enacted and not thought about too deeply. Lady Macbeth reaffirms Macbeth's lack of sleep, and he acknowledges the psychological effect his sleep depravity has had on his emotional state, noting that, at times, he is behaving like a novice, instead of the seasoned warrior he knows himself to be.

Scene 5: Very Witchy, but Middleton's Imprint Is Most Suspic-y

Because of the prominence of the character Hecate and because of the insertion of a song from the play *The Witch*, many scholars surmise that Thomas Middleton, not William Shakespeare, composed this scene (Muir, 1992). The reader or viewer hears a frustrated Hecate admonishing the other three witches for conversing with Macbeth and not including her: "And I, the mistress of your charms, / The close contriver of all harms, / Was never called to bear my part / Or show the glory of our art?" (III. v. 6–9).

ACTIVITY: RESEARCH

Research the controversy surrounding Thomas Middleton's "contribution" to *Macbeth*. Review what scholars say about Act III, scene v, and Act IV, scene i.

Scene 6: Lennox Plays the Greek Chorus

Sequentially, this scene most likely was placed here rather than after Act IV, scene i, because the insertion of Hecate in Act III, scene v, would have resulted in two juxtaposed witch scenes (Muir, 1992). Nevertheless, in this scene Lennox represents the prevailing attitude of the nobility in Scotland. Lennox speaks to another Lord, who could be Angus (Muir, 1992). Lennox observes that there appears to be a pattern of sons killing fathers in Scotland of late: Malcolm and Donalbain killing Duncan and fleeing and Fleance killing Banquo and fleeing, too. Lennox reviews Macbeth's emotional reaction to Duncan's murder. "How it did grieve Macbeth! Did he not straight / In pious rage the two delinquents tear / That were the slaves of drink and thralls of sleep?" (III. vi. 12–14).

Next, the tone of Lennox's speech shifts, "Was not that nobly done? Ay, and wisely, too" (III. vi. 15). He continues his sarcasm with an observation: "That had he [Macbeth] Duncan's sons under his key / (As, an 't please heaven, he shall not) they should / find / What 'twere to kill a father. So should Fleance" (III. vi. 19–22). Lennox's loyalty is now in question, as is the Lord with whom he converses.

The dialogue shifts to Macduff's decision not to attend Macbeth's coronation feast. Also, the Lord explains that Malcolm has been granted refuge from Edward, the King of England, and Macduff is seeking military support from King Edward and hoping the king persuades Northumberland and Siward to help seat the rightful person, Malcolm, on Scotland's throne.

Macbeth, according to the Lord, is aware of Malcolm and Macduff's plan and prepares Scotland for war. On behalf of Macbeth, a messenger invites Macduff to meet with him. Of course, Macduff refuses. The Lord reports the messenger's thoughts: "'You'll rue the time / That clogs me with this answer'" (III. vi. 47–48). The messenger realizes that Macbeth does not want to hear bad news, and, as the Elizabethan, Jacobean, and modern theater-goer knows, a messenger has an occupational hazard component included with his employment. That is, the possibility of delivering bad news and then dying for it occurs at the whim of the king.

Like a Greek chorus, Lennox analyzes the current events of the play, reflecting on the plot and the characters involved in the major decisions of the plot structure. He is pensive, revealing that he initially supported Macbeth, but has changed his mind as the horrors of the despot's reign unfolds.

ACTIVITY: RESEARCH

Research the function of the Greek chorus in the classical period. Report the role and responsibility of the chorus. Consider Lennox's role in this scene and determine whether or not he serves the same role in this play.

Act IV: Sleepless Nights and Evil Spirits

Scene 1: Something Wicked This Way Comes

To distinguish the supernatural quality of the witches from the nobility, Shakespeare has the Weïrd Sisters speak in a trochaic tetrameter rhyme scheme. Consider: "Double, double toil and trouble; / Fire burn, and cauldron bubble" (IV. i. 10–11). A *trochee* with its stress on the first syllable is the opposite in structure of an iamb, which stresses the second syllable. Counting the syllables in the witches' speech, the careful reader will observe seven syllables. The prosodic structure of the individual witch's chants that follow is written in a catalectic or truncated form of trochaic tetrameter with a line missing a syllable in the last foot (Baer, 2006).

Odd numbers were needed for magical events, so the second witch repeats what the first witch says and starts counting again (Muir, 1992): "Thrice the brinded cat hath mewed. / Thrice, and once the hedge-pig whined" (IV. i. 1–2).

The witches acknowledge their "familiar" as read in the beginning of the play. The familiar is "an attendant spirit" serving a witch in the form of an animal (Mowat & Werstine, 2004, p. 6). Graymalkin, Paddock, and Harpier are the first, second, and third witches' familiars, respectively (Mowat & Werstine, 2004). To meet audience expectation, Shakespeare places the setting in a house with the witches in front of a cauldron. The witches toss various items into the bubbling brew, beginning with a poisoned toad.

Each item has a particular evil connotation. For example, "Root of hemlock digged i' th' dark" (IV. i. 25) includes a time factor. Herbs dug in the dark would have more potency. The references to Jew, Turk, and Tartar have higher witch value because all are not christened (Muir, 1992). Hecate's entrance (IV. i. 39–43) and the following "Black Spirit" song from the play *The Witches* suggest another non-Shakespearean interpolation.

Ironically, the witches identify Macbeth as "Something wicked this way comes" after hearing his knocking (IV. i. 45). The second witch's remark illuminates how rapidly Macbeth's stature has declined. Macbeth reinforces a common belief among Elizabethans/Jacobeans that witches had control over the winds. The Church of England certainly would maintain that God had authority over nature's forces. Macbeth's quotation, "Though you untie the winds and let them fight / Against the churches" (IV. i. 53–54), would be accepted by Jacobean audiences as a truism.

Macbeth continues his demands to know his future with myriad examples of destruction: "Though castles topple on their warders' heads, / [. . .] though the treasure / Of nature's germens tumble all together / Even till destruction sicken, answer me / To what I ask you" (IV. i. 58–64). Shakespeare includes personification in the speech's closing line. "Destruction sicken" (IV. i. 63) means that even if there is massive chaos and confusion until nature is nauseated with the monstrous result, he, Macbeth, must know his future (Muir, 1992).

Apparitions appear with symbolic meaning. First, the armed head foreshadows the outcome of Macbeth's eventual fight with Macduff, the Thane of Fife. The second apparition represents Macduff as a Caesarian-delivered baby, and the third apparition symbolizes Malcolm, the future king of Scotland, who orders tree branches from Birnam Wood to be hewed as camouflage for the soldiers attacking Macbeth's castle on Dunsinane Hill.

ACTIVITY: INTERPRETIVE ESSAY

Interpret the statements of the three apparitions. Macbeth views the apparitions' proclamations as helpful advice. Why? How does Macbeth interpret the remarks? What do you believe they mean?

After the spirits conclude, Macbeth responds in the same rhyming pattern as the evil apparitions. His humanity continues to diminish. Taking a moment of solace in his interpretation of the evil spirits' predictions, Macbeth maintains his purpose for the visit: "Tell me, if your art / Can tell so much: shall Banquo's issue ever / Reign in this kingdom?" (IV. i. 115–117). The witches show Macbeth a line of kings descended from Banquo. The image of the glass is the Elizabethan/Jacobean interpretation of two mirrors facing each other to indicate infinity.

Lennox appears after the witches vanish. Reinforcing the Elizabethan/Jacobean belief that the Weïrd Sisters have powers to evaporate, Lennox says that he saw nothing or no one pass him. Because Macbeth is so consumed with his own provincial outlook, he does not comprehend the irony of his reaction: "Infected be the air whereon they ride, / And damned all those that trust them!" (IV. i. 157–158). Moments before Lennox's entrance, Banquo's ghost raises a mirror to reveal a line of kings symbolically stretching forever. Perhaps Macbeth should look in it, because he just "damned" himself. Lennox reports, "Macduff is fled to England" (IV. i. 161), information that Lennox already learned from an unnamed lord in Act III, scene vi, lines 33–35. Macbeth resolves to seize Macduff's castle and kill everyone in it. In his aside he is determined to act and not to think: "The very firstlings of my heart shall be / The firstlings of my hand" (IV. i. 167–168). He repeats this idea to himself. That is, the thought must transform into the deed.

Scene 2: Who Is the Mysterious Messenger?

Ross, who functions primarily as a messenger in the play, unsuccessfully tries to explain the reason for Macduff's departure to Lady Macduff. Some critics have proposed that Macduff has discussed his leaving for England, and Lady Macduff, unsure of Ross' loyalty, denounces her husband to shift any possible complicity from herself (Muir, 1992). Remember, Macbeth did reveal, "in [Macduff's] house / I keep a servant fee'd" (III. iv. 163–164). One may surmise that spying is a "de rigueur" practice recognized by the citizens of Macbeth's Scotland. Conversely, Lady Macduff may not have thought her life was in danger. Also, from what we learn about Macduff in his conversation with Malcolm, Macduff would not have left had he thought his family would be in any danger from the tyrant Macbeth.

Presenting these two alternatives should encourage classroom discussion. Consider waiting until after the Macduff-Malcolm dialogue exchange in Act IV, scene iii. The students will have a more informed impression of Macduff's character after the next scene.

ACTIVITY: INTERPRETIVE ESSAY—MACDUFF

Is Macduff a coward for leaving his family? Consider his viewpoint and assess Lady Macduff's viewpoint. Why would he leave his wife and son behind and travel to Scotland? What does Macbeth gain from killing Macduff's family?

Ross unsuccessfully tries to explain to Lady Macduff that her husband is well schooled in the current political climate: he "best knows / The fits o' th' season" (IV. ii. 19–20). Ross says Macduff left for reasons other than cowardice. Hoping to return when the political climate is better, Ross says, "[I] Shall not be long but I'll be here again" (IV. ii. 27). Extending Ross' (and her husband's) view that there is no danger, Lady Macduff talks to her son about his father abandoning them. The son is asked how will he live, and bird metaphors follow. The son says, "Poor birds they are not set / for" (IV. ii. 42–43). Perhaps this remark acknowledges incorrectly that they are not in danger, but Lady Macduff still calls her husband a traitor (IV. ii. 51–52). "Lady Macduff defines a traitor as one who swears an oath of loyalty to a sovereign and then breaks it" (Mowat & Werstine, 2004, p. 134). Macduff very clearly affirms his loyalty to his homeland by refusing to attend Macbeth's coronation and leaving Scotland to seek out Malcolm.

ACTIVITY: INTERPRETIVE ESSAY—LADY MACDUFF

Consider: Does Lady Macduff mean her husband or Macbeth when she defines traitor in Act IV, scene ii, lines 51–70?

A messenger enters to urge Lady Macduff to get out of the castle immediately. The messenger acknowledges Lady Macduff's stature and apologizes for frightening her, but the messenger says to remain silent, when danger is imminent, is even more cruel: "To do worse to you were fell cruelty, / Which is too nigh your person" (IV. ii. 77–78).

ACTIVITY: SMALL-GROUP DISCUSSION

Speculate with your students about the messenger. Who could the messenger be? Explore all of the options, referencing character, plot, setting, and conflict.

Lady Macduff laments the strangeness of her world now "where to do harm / Is often laudable, to do good sometime / Accounted dangerous folly" (IV. ii. 83–85). The murderers enter and kill Macduff's family.

Scene 3: O, Scotland!—Where Vices Are Virtues and Virtues Vices

In this scene Macduff, unaware of his family's demise, meets with Malcolm, the designated heir to Scotland's throne. Wary of Macduff, Malcolm says, "You have loved him well. / He hath not touched you yet" (IV. iii. 15–16). From Malcolm's view Macduff appears to be allied with Macbeth, so the initial comments from Malcolm reflect his suspicions: "Though all things foul would wear the brows of / grace, / Yet grace must still look so" (IV. iii. 28–30). In addition, Malcolm naturally wonders why Macduff would leave his family unprotected. Malcolm suspects that Macduff is one of the many spies Macbeth sends to lure Malcolm back to Scotland.

Insulted, Macduff stands up to leave. "Fare thee well, lord. / I would not be the villain that thou think'st / For the whole space that's in the tyrant's grasp" (IV. iii. 43–45). Malcolm tries to assuage Macduff's feelings by noting that each day brings reports of Macbeth's abuses and actions by their countrymen to defeat Macbeth: "And here from gracious England have I offer / Of goodly thousands" (IV. iii. 53–54). Malcolm reports that his host, Edward the Confessor, has pledged thousands of soldiers.

Macduff's Loyalty Test

To test Macduff's loyalty, Malcolm proclaims that Scotland under his rule will suffer more than under Macbeth's reign: "black Macbeth / Will seem as pure as snow, and the poor state / Esteem him as a lamb, being compared / With my confineless harms" (IV. iii. 63–66). Of course, Macduff does not believe that anyone could be more evil than Macbeth: "Not in the legions / Of horrid hell can come a devil more damned / In evils to top Macbeth" (IV. iii. 67–69).

ACTIVITY: CRITICAL READING—MALCOLM'S VICES

On a separate sheet of paper, type the speeches by Malcolm where he lists his vices. Instruct the students to read through the speeches, noting the flaws Malcolm indicates to be unworthy of a king (see IV. iii. 70–79, 91–99). In addition, define the kingly virtues Malcolm addresses (see IV. iii. 107–116). Furthermore, direct the class to review Macduff's responses to the litany of vices.

The Right Stuff?

Macduff banishes himself from Scotland, seeing no hope for its recovery (IV. iii. 130–132). His sincere response convinces Malcolm that he is a true patriot. Malcolm repudiates all of his vices as a test, confessing that he is the opposite of that which he said. One topic for class discussion or written composition might be to debate whether or not Malcolm is the right choice to replace Macbeth. Review Malcolm's speech in Act IV, scene iii, lines 133–156 where he reveals his inexperience with women, leadership, and battle. Is he worthy enough to be king?

The doctor enters. Muir (1992) interprets the interruption as a chance to "flatter James I with its reference to a good supernatural in Edward compared to an evil supernatural with the Weïrd Sisters" (p. 130). Malcolm explains to Macduff that Edward has the power to cure "the evil," a form of tuberculosis (IV. iii. 168). The king hangs a necklace with a stamped coin to cure the sick in Act IV, scene iii, lines 175–178.

Following this interlude, Ross enters with tragic news for Macduff. Shakespeare develops a depth of character and conflict in Ross as a bearer of heartrending news. Note how he hesitates to report his purpose, commenting indirectly initially. Macduff, in disbelief, repeats what he just heard: "My children too?" (IV. iii. 248) and "My wife killed too?" (IV. iii. 250). Malcolm advises Macduff to take "great revenge / To cure this deadly grief" (IV. iii. 253–254).

Then Macduff says, "He has no children" (IV. iii. 255). Consider the pronoun here. Does Macduff mean Malcolm who has no children and who advocates revenge for replacing grief? Or, does he refer to Macbeth, who, having no children, would never have ordered a child's murder had he had children of his own. Muir (1992) suggested another option: Macbeth, not having any children, will never be able to suffer an equal revenge. After Malcolm says, "Dispute it like a man" (IV. iii. 259), Macduff responds that he "must also feel it as a man" (IV. iii. 261).

The act concludes with Malcolm saying that the time to end Macbeth's reign is now: "Our power is ready; / Our lack is nothing but our leave" (IV. iii. 277–278).

Act V: Enemies at the Gate
and Macduff's Cure for Scotland

Scene 1: Lady Macbeth Can't Get the Red Out

The gentlewoman says that Lady Macbeth has been walking in her sleep since her husband "went into the field" (V. i. 4). This observation supports Ross' report to Malcolm that he saw "the tyrant's power afoot" (IV. iii. 214). Muir (1992) commented that Macbeth, prior to the English invasion, would have ordered his troops to seek out and kill any rebel forces.

Nevertheless, the doctor concludes that one's mind must be in a state of great agitation while simultaneously experiencing the benefits of sleep and performing the actions of a person who is awake. The gentlewoman is reluctant to share Lady Macbeth's utterances with the doctor. There is an atmosphere of distrust in the castle, and the gentlewoman's hesitancy is understandable. She says, "Neither to you nor anyone, having no / witness to confirm my speech" (V. i. 19–20). After all, the gentlewoman would be accusing the Queen of Scotland of murder.

"Out, Damned Spot! Out, I Say"

As Lady Macbeth speaks, the doctor writes down her unconscious confession. He says, "I will set down what comes / from her, to satisfy my remembrance the more / strongly" (V. i. 34–36). Lady Macbeth's "Out, damned spot, out, I say!" (V. i. 37) remarks recall the sequence of events on the night of Duncan's murder. Beginning with the blood on her hands, she then observes the time: "One. Two. / Why then, 'tis time to do 't" (V. i. 37–38). Next, reinforcing her fear of the dark and her acknowledgement of the severity and consequence of her crime, she says, "Hell is murky" (V. i. 38). Following this point, she reveals her impatience with her husband's hesitancy to return the daggers back to Duncan's chamber: "Fie, my / lord, fie, a soldier and afeard?" (V. i. 38–39). Reflecting the attitude of a tyrant, Lady Macbeth says, "What need we fear / who knows it, when none can call our power to / account?" (V. i. 39–41). Lady Macbeth refers to a time in the play when she was not queen; yet, she takes the view that she and Macbeth are above the law and not accountable for their actions. Observe how she realizes that she is held responsible by God and not by man. Her last line about blood in Act V, scene i, line 42 denotes the actual murder of the king, startling the gentlewoman and the doctor.

> ## ACTIVITY: CRITICAL READING—
> ## LADY MACBETH'S SLEEPWALKING
>
> Review the "Out, damned spot" speech. What do the remarks reveal about Lady Macbeth's character? Interpret each line for meaning, citing other lines in the play to place her remarks in context.

Next, Lady Macbeth makes an unexpected observation about Lady Macduff and Macduff. Because Lady Macbeth's initial prayer to the evil spirits to "Stop up th' access and passage to remorse" (I. v. 51) is not working, her reference to Lady Macduff is intriguing. In her burgeoning guilt is it possible that she tries to prevent Lady Macduff's murder? Consider the evidence. In this scene she mentions that "The Thane of Fife had a wife. Where is / she now?" (V. i. 44–45). Her sleepwalking ritual includes a pantomime of a person writing a letter. Is this letter a warning delivered by a messenger or is Lady Macbeth, the messenger in disguise, assuaging her ever-growing guilt?

Note the meaning of the doctor's "Go to, go to" line as shame (V. i. 48; Mowat & Werstine, 2004, p. 162). The doctor is addressing Lady Macbeth, not the gentlewoman. The scene concludes with Lady Macbeth confessing about Banquo and the doctor revealing the larger geopolitical consequences of the Macbeths' alleged actions when "Foul whisp'rings are abroad" (V. i. 75). He also tells the gentlewoman to "Look after her [Lady Macbeth]. / Remove from her the means of all annoyance / And still keep eyes upon her" (V. i. 79–81). The doctor foreshadows Lady Macbeth's suicide here, determining that she needs a minister more than a doctor: "More needs she the divine than the physician" (V. i. 78). Also, living under an atmosphere of distrust, the doctor closes the scene with a remark that says that what he witnessed will not be shared with anyone: "I think but dare not speak" (V. i. 83).

Scene 2: Scottish Rebels Meet the English for Tea, Scones, and Macbeth's Demise

The significance of this scene is immediately apparent with the alliance between the Scottish rebels, comprising Menteith, Caithness, Angus, and Lennox; and the English forces, with Siward and his son, accompanying Malcolm and Macduff. Lennox's joining the rebels is evidence of the growing dissension among Scottish nobles toward Macbeth's regime. Remember, Lennox was among the nobles joining Macbeth at his celebratory banquet that went awry when Banquo's ghost appeared. Lennox says to Caithness that he has a list of the nobles who have joined their cause and Donalbain is not on the list.

ACTIVITY: CREATIVE WRITING—DONALBAIN

Have the students determine the reason for Donalbain's decision not to join the rebels against Macbeth. Students may create a dialogue between Donalbain and Malcolm or compose a descriptive piece explicating his decision to remain in Ireland. Another option is to have your students model Shakespeare's style and compose the dialogue in iambic pentameter.

The next exchange of dialogue between Caithness and Angus includes two famous clothing metaphors. First, Caithness, in referencing Macbeth, says, "He cannot buckle his distempered cause / Within the belt of rule" (V. ii. 17–18). Angus responds, "Now does he feel his title / Hang loose about him, like a giant's robe / Upon a dwarfish thief" (V. ii. 23–25). Each comparison comments on how ill suited Macbeth is to lead Scotland. Shakespeare returns to the bloody hands imagery with Angus observing that Macbeth feels "His secret murders sticking on his hands" (V. ii. 20). Also, leading into the clothing metaphor, Angus says, "Those he commands move only in command, / Nothing in love" (V. ii. 22–23). The motivation for those troops fighting for Macbeth is only the false king's threats. Unlike them, the Scottish nobles want "To give obedience where 'tis truly owed" (V. ii. 31).

ACTIVITY: METAPHORS AND SIMILES

Using the clothing metaphors listed above, have the students create other metaphors to describe Macbeth's reign. Students may work alone or in pairs. Share the results with the class.

Caithness says, "Meet we the med'cine of the sickly weal, / And with him pour we in our country's purge / Each drop of us" (V. ii. 32–34). The Scottish noblemen are prepared to join Malcolm, the "med'cine," and give their lives to rid Scotland of Macbeth.

Scene 3: Ten Thousand at the Door; No One Loves Me Anymore

Inside Dunsinane, Macbeth's agitation at the impending English invasion increases. By focusing on the spirits' prophecies, he attempts to assuage his concern: "The spirits that know / All mortal consequences have pronounced me thus: / 'Fear not, Macbeth. No man that's born of woman / Shall e'er have power upon thee'" (V. iii. 4–7). He dismisses the loss of support among the Scottish thanes, telling them to "mingle with the English epicures" (V. iii. 8). The Scottish people had little knowledge of fine fare and dismissed the "superfluous gormandizing brought in by the Englishmen" (Muir, 1992, p. 144).

When a servant enters to give Macbeth information about the English invasion, the servant is insulted: "What soldiers, patch? / What soldiers, whey-face?" (V. iii. 18, 20). Patch is a term of derision, perhaps derived from the king's fool who wore a multicolored coat (Muir, 1992). Macbeth's soliloquy acknowledges his increasing awareness of his fragile hold on the throne and his impending death: "My way of life / Is fall'n into the sere, the yellow leaf, / And that which should accompany old age, / As honor, love, obedience, troops of friends, / I must not look to have" (V. iii. 26–30).

> ## ACTIVITY: CRITICAL READING—CHARACTER INTERPRETATION
>
> Read Macbeth's soliloquy (V. iii. 24–33) closely. What do you deduce about Macbeth from his remarks? Cite lines to support your interpretation.

Dismissing the servant, Macbeth calls for Seyton to help him with his armor. Students often confuse the name with Satan. Actually, "the Setons of Touch were hereditary armour-bearers to the Kings of Scotland" (Muir, 1992, p. 146). Consider the action in the scene and note what task Seyton performs. Also, Seyton confirms the reports about the invasion.

A doctor enters while Seyton is putting on Macbeth's armor and Macbeth inquires about the health of Lady Macbeth. The doctor explains that her emotional distress is preventing her from resting properly: "Not so sick, my lord, / As she is troubled with thick-coming fancies / That keep her from her rest" (V. iii. 46–48). Macbeth mixes the topic of curing his wife to wondering if the doctor could "cast / The water of my land" (V. iii. 62–63), that is, diagnose Scotland's ills.

Scene 4: The Walking Trees of Birnam Wood

The Scottish forces join the English at Birnam Wood. Malcolm recalls the murder of his father: "I hope the days are near at hand / That chambers will be safe" (V. iv. 1–2). He demonstrates some military acumen by ordering each soldier to "hew him down a bough / And bear 't before him" (V. iv. 6–7). He notes that the illusion it creates will camouflage the number of troops when Macbeth views Birnam Wood from Dunsinane Castle. Malcolm opines that Macbeth has lost support among nobles and commoners: "Both more and less have given him the revolt" (V. iv. 16). Siward, however, cautions Malcolm that rumors about the morale of Macbeth's troops will be determined on the battlefield: "Thoughts speculative their unsure hopes relate, / But certain issue strokes must arbitrate" (V. iv. 25–26).

Scene 5: Tomorrow and Tomorrow and Tomorrow

The scene opens with Macbeth confidently prepared to counter the invaders. He remarks, "Were they not forced with those that should be / ours, / We might have met them direful, beard to beard" (V. v. 5–7). He acknowledges that the English forces received a boost from the Scottish rebels. His thoughts are interrupted by a scream. Seyton reports that Lady Macbeth has died. Macbeth's response leads to the most famous speech of the play.

Initially, Macbeth's response appears callous: "She should have died hereafter. / There would have been a time for such a word" (V. v. 20–21). In other words, her death, like all deaths, was inevitable; however, her timing is particularly inconvenient. Following this remark, Macbeth expresses his nihilistic point of view about the meaninglessness of existence. He sees each day as the same: "Tomorrow and tomorrow and tomorrow / Creeps in this petty pace from day to day / To the last syllable of recorded time" (V. v. 22–24). Perhaps Shakespeare was influenced by Job 18:6 when he wrote, "And all our yesterdays have lighted fools / The way to dusty death. Out, out, brief candle!" (V. v. 25–26). The Job verse reads "The light shall be dark in his tabernacle, and his candle shall be put out with him." Each image reinforces the brevity of existence.

Continuing, Macbeth shifts metaphors to a stage where an actor has his moment and is gone: "Life's but a walking shadow, a poor player / That struts and frets his hour upon the stage / And then is heard no more" (V. v. 27–29). Shakespeare's description of a "poor player" indicates audience sympathy toward the actor for his brief appearance on life's stage, not his economic status. Furthermore, Macbeth closes his pessimistic view with "It is a tale / Told by an idiot, full of sound and fury, / Signifying nothing" (V. v. 29–31). Once again, Shakespeare may have been influenced by a biblical verse, Psalms 90:9: "For all our days are passed away in thy wrath: we spend our years as a tale that is told."

A messenger enters, reporting that the woods appear to be moving. Of course, Macbeth is incredulous upon hearing this news and says, "I pull in resolution and begin / To doubt th' equivocation of the fiend, / That lies like truth" (V. v. 48–50). His confidence wanes with this news. Macbeth recalls the spirit's warning about Birnam Wood coming toward Dunsinane Hill.

Scene 6: Arrival at Dunsinane

Malcolm orders Siward and his son to enter the castle first. He points out that he and Macduff shall perform tasks worthy of their status. As the Folger Shakespeare Library edition note indicates, Malcolm does refer to himself in the royal "we" (Mowat & Werstine, 2004, p. 180). Malcolm chooses to stay back, putting Siward and his son in harm's way.

ACTIVITY: CLASS DISCUSSION/ ONE-PARAGRAPH RESPONSE

Comment on Malcolm's decision to send the battle-tested Siward and his young son into Macbeth's castle first. As the future leader of Scotland, should Malcolm be delegating authority or leading the charge into the castle himself?

Scene 7: Not Born of Woman

Outside his castle Macbeth kills Siward's son. Prior to his fight with young Siward, Macbeth envisions himself surrounded like a bear in a bear baiting contest, a sport enjoyed by the English of this time period. A *course* in Act V, scene vii, line 2 "meant a round between a bear and the attack dogs" (Muir, 1992, p. 156).

Desperately searching for Macbeth, Macduff says that he must find him or his "wife and children's ghosts will haunt me still" (V. vii. 21). Macduff does not want to fight the "wretched kerns, whose arms / Are hired to bear their staves" (V. vii. 22–23). Macbeth and Banquo were sent by Duncan at the beginning of the play to squash the rebellion led by Macdonwald, who hired Irish mercenaries to help his cause. Ironically, Macbeth has hired the kerns to help him fight against Malcolm.

ACTIVITY: POWERPOINT PRESENTATION ON BEAR BAITING

Assign a short research paper on bear baiting. To vary the topics, consider looking at the games and sports of the Elizabethan and Jacobean periods.

Siward announces that the castle has fallen under Malcolm's command without any significant resistance. Malcolm enters the castle and acknowledges Siward's report that Macbeth's forces are deserting: "We have met with foes / That strike beside us" (V. vii. 34–35).

Scene 8: Macduff's Cure for a Headache

The scene opens with Macbeth discounting any notion of suicide. Macduff finally sees Macbeth on the battlefield. In an unusual departure from his boasting behavior, Macbeth tells Macduff to stay back because "My soul is too much charged / With blood of thine already" (V. viii. 6–7). Of course, Macduff seeks vengeance and they fight. Again, Macbeth warns Macduff to retreat because "I bear a charmèd life, which must not yield / To one of woman born" (V. viii. 15–16). Macduff says, "let the angel whom thou hast served / Tell thee Macduff was from his mother's womb / Untimely ripped" (V. viii. 18–20). By not being delivered through the birth canal, and, because his mother died in childbirth, Macduff, in the evil spirit's sense, is not of woman born.

Macbeth drops his sword after cursing the ambiguity of the evil spirit's misleading words. Macduff only accepts Macbeth's yielding if he agrees "to be the show and gaze o' th' time" (V. viii. 28). Macbeth, Macduff says, will be treated like "our rarer monsters are, / Painted upon a pole" (V. viii. 29–30). Macbeth's choice: To be mocked as a sideshow freak or to fight. He chooses to fight.

ACTIVITY: VISUAL

Have the students draw or sculpt an image of Macduff's plan for Macbeth, if he chooses not to fight Macduff.

With Macbeth and Macduff fighting off stage, the action shifts back to the castle, where Malcolm and Siward are joined by Ross, thanes, and soldiers. Ross, in his role of messenger again, delivers sad news to Siward that his son died in battle. Macduff enters carrying Macbeth's head on a pole: "Behold where stands / Th' usurper's cursèd head" (V. viii. 65–66). Macduff hails Malcolm as king and praises the Scottish thanes surrounding the new king: "I see thee compassed with thy kingdom's pearl" (V. viii. 67). To reward his noble supporters, Malcolm creates the position of earl, a position in the English hierarchy that ranks above that of thane. Also, it is a position that includes a hereditary promise for future generations.

Rethinking Character: The Human Nature of Villainy

"I think nothing equals Macbeth. It is wonderful."
Abraham Lincoln (August 17, 1863)

On the evening of August 7, 1606, King James I and his brother-in-law King Christian IV of Denmark sat in Hampton Court and watched the inaugural production of William Shakespeare's *Macbeth*. Unlike his predecessor, Elizabeth I, James I often was disengaged from theatrical productions and frankly preferred to be hunting or maybe even sleeping than to attend a dramatic performance. Yet, this play, penned by William Shakespeare, one of James' King's Men, was different. This engaging tale was about a historical king from Scotland named Macbeth. The production filled the dark recesses of Hampton Court with accounts of Scottish history, images of bloodshed, scenes of sleepwalking, and witches' cauldrons that were filled with gruesome items. These likenesses caused the normally disinterested James to take notice and revel in the sheer magnificence of this production.

When the first folio was printed in 1623, and the script of "The Scottish Play" was replicated for the world to read, Jacobeans did not know what to make of the apparently evil Macbeth. Even today, when students encounter *Macbeth* for the first time, they are led to believe that the eponymous character is purely evil, and that his ambition and his lack of backbone in listening to Lady Macbeth and the witches are the causes of his undoing. Yet, there is much more to his character than meets the eye.

Ask professional actors what the defining role of a male actor's career should be, and most will resoundingly agree that successfully enacting Shakespeare's young Prince Hamlet is the line of demarcation between a mediocre actor and a great leading man. Many actors share that the role of Hamlet, comprising emotional peaks and valleys, challenges even the most veteran actor. It would appear that portraying Macbeth, however, lacks the challenges and complexity of many other Shakespearean protagonists, even the most evil and vile. The title of the play and the very role of the Scottish usurper are filled with historical superstitions and generally bad luck. Does the "purely" evil nature of Macbeth dissuade great actors? Many famous actors have portrayed Macbeth: the 17th-century's Richard Burbage and the 18th century's David Garrick; the 19th century's William Charles Macready, Samuel Phelps, and Charles Kean; the 20th century's Orson Welles and Lawrence Olivier; and the 21st-century's Patrick Stewart all have played the lead role. Although the portrayal of Macbeth does not rank as a necessity for actors, as an epic role that defines an actor's career, it is still a favorite of many theatergoers. Interestingly, a number of historians have cited *Macbeth* as a favorite play of Abraham Lincoln, and, in an ironic twist, in 1863, 2 years prior to assassinating Lincoln, John Wilkes Booth portrayed Macbeth on stage.

As a classroom play for high school students, *Macbeth* is one of Shakespeare's shortest tragedies, 29 scenes in five acts, and approximately 2,108 lines. Unlike longer plays with varying degrees of complexity such as *Hamlet* and *King Lear*, *Macbeth* appears to be a very straightforward account of a man's downward spiral toward self-destruction. Macbeth's obvious malevolence and villainy paint him as a simplistic murderer, akin to the fatalistic characters of medieval morality plays who choose evil and eternal damnation over goodness. Other Shakespearean villains may require a much deeper analysis and have far greater complexity. A novice reader of the play may observe that this lack of depth is an apparent deficiency in Macbeth's character. Yet, nothing could be further from the truth.

Comparing Literary Villains to Macbeth

One such multifaceted character that frequently provides students with a number of interpretations is the character of Iago in *Othello*. The villainous Iago is one of the cruelest and most vile characters in the English language. There is no clear rationale why Iago manipulates and connives to destroy the characters in the play. Clearly, the most obvious reason is due to Othello's fateful decision to pass over Iago for the role of captain in favor of the younger and less experienced Michael Cassio. Yet, Iago's revenge extends to all who get in his path of revenge including but not limited to Othello and Cassio. At the play's conclusion, the audience is left to wonder what Iago's true rationale has been for murder. In a uniquely Shakespearean twist, the character of Iago remains silent about his treacherous motivations, and the audience is left unfulfilled at the play's conclusion. (Iago, unlike other Shakespearean villains, remains mute and is alive at the end of the play, but the audience is lead to surmise that he most likely will be tortured and executed in the coming days).

In a similarly deceptive manner, the character of Claudius from *Hamlet* kills his eldest brother and marries his sister-in-law in order to attain the Danish crown. Only through the mass destruction of the poisoned fencing match in Act V, scene ii of the play (with the nudging of the ghost of the elder Hamlet to his son) is Claudius ironically defeated by his own treachery. Another such vile Shakespearean creation is the tyrannical Richard III from the play *Richard III*. Physically deformed and morally corrupt, Richard III executes anyone who is an impediment to his kingly aspirations. Richard III's death, at the hands of Richmond at the Battle of Bosworth Field, draws to a close The War of the Roses. Similar to Iago and Richard III, the evil character of Edmund, the illegitimate child of Gloucester from *King Lear*, seeks to destroy his half-brother, Edgar, and their father to acquire their possessions and titles. Edmund's plot to destroy his family and, ultimately, to usurp the throne of Lear climaxes with the murder of the king's daughter, Cordelia. Just as in all Elizabethan/Jacobean tragedy, order is restored to the kingdom when Edgar vanquishes him.

Macbeth's alienation from the world, based on his own perversion of the world order of Scotland, is better compared to Christopher Marlowe's Doctor Faustus and John Milton's Satan from *Paradise Lost*. Each character rejects his traditional role to ascend to a higher position in society: Faustus wants all of the knowledge in the world; the fallen angel Satan desires to be God's equal; and Macbeth seeks the position that he cannot achieve without violent means.

The Original "He Who Must Not Be Named"

"Macbeth!" If we were in a play rehearsal at this moment, and someone spoke this name aloud, there would be a very uncomfortable pause and maybe even some type of punishment for the speaker to serve in order to set things right again in the theater atmosphere that he or she so unknowingly disturbed.

What an odd practice! What is the story behind the curse of "The Scottish Play" and why do so many people associate the name of the play with the most ubiquitous theater curse? To ward off this curse, some people call it "The Scottish Play," "The Comedy of Glamis," "That Play," or "The Scottish Tragedy." Others force the violator of this cardinal rule to perform one of the "prescribed purifying rituals" (Garber, 2008, p. 89) after chasing the guilty party off the stage. In order to return to the stage, the actor must either turn three times, spit over one's left shoulder, spout obscenities, or recite from *The Merchant of Venice* or *Hamlet* to somehow "exorcize" the theater where the production is rehearsing (Garber, 2008). Great actors who play the titular roles of Macbeth and Lady Macbeth choose to refer to their play and character as "Mr. and Mrs. M" and wholeheartedly refuse to name *Macbeth* in the theater.

Why is this done? Is it the witches at the beginning of the production that have so attached wickedness to the play? *Hamlet*, for example, begins with the ghost of Hamlet's father; yet, there is no negative association with this play.

There are some very pragmatic reasons why the play may have acquired a very superstitious following. One such reason is that after many theater companies had finished its run of the play, the playhouse would close down shortly after its last production of *Macbeth*. This action may be true of some playhouses; however, when a bit of investigation is completed in this area, one realizes that these playhouses closed (or were planning to close) regardless of what the final play turned out to be. *Macbeth*, always a popular and accessible drama for audiences because it is filled with witches and bloodshed, would have filled the theater's seats, anyway.

A second more practical reason would be the dark stage settings and smoke-filled ambience in the theater. In such cramped quarters and with a number of sword fights built into the plot, injuries are a natural consequence of the production and its props and set design.

Yet, what about the validity of this curse? There is a very superstitious history to *Macbeth*—we can safely say the name because, at the time of this writing, we are neither in a theater nor acting in a production of the play—and, as any student of drama knows, actors by their very nature are superstitious. The history of the curse is given a very thorough and extensive treatment in an article entitled "The Curse of the Play" by Robert Faires (2000), which reproduced each of the many curses and odd histories that surround the play. We highly recommend this article to educators and students who would be interested in "the curse." Perhaps a writing exercise investigating the origin of these stories may be a worthwhile research option as an extension activity. Although the facts behind many of these tales associated with the play are fabricated and embellished or based on mere coincidence, some others may not be. We leave it for you to be the judge. Remember, do *not* say the name of the play in a theater!

Unambiguous Evil

So, what villainous intricacies exist at the heart of the Thane of Glamis/Thane of Cawdor/King of Scotland? Why does he decide to commit regicide and become the usurper King of Scotland? It does not appear that the trappings of kingship and a growing avarice for kingly trimmings overwhelm his sense of right and wrong. So, why does he do it? According to *A Preface to Shakespeare's Tragedies* (Mangan, 1991):

The killings that Macbeth carries out, either directly or indirectly, have no ambiguity about them. He is under no compulsion or misapprehension as he murders, or orders the murders of Duncan, Banquo and Lady Macduff and her children. He may feel guilt, terror, despair and even occasional remorse, but we are never asked to see any of them as justifiable homicide. They are acts of unambiguous evil. (p. 189)

Yet, the killings and the killer are not so easily dismissed. The more wretched he becomes, the more quickly critical readers of *Macbeth* become drawn to him. We struggle to ascertain how and why he becomes the nihilistic monster into which he morphs by Act V; consequently, do we feel an emotional disengagement from this fiendlike hero-villain?

From our first introduction to Macbeth, he is the archetypal hero, the man who takes on entire armies with blood-wet weapons and slices through enemies "from the nave to th' chops" (I. ii. 24) like a critic skewering a poorly performed play. As a witness to the story told by the Captain in Act I, scene ii of the play, similar to the epic poetry construct of *in medias res*, Macbeth wreaks such havoc on the battlefield that he effectively salvages the battle for the Scots, to "memorize another Golgotha" (I. ii. 45) and plays the role of "Bellona's bridegroom" (I. ii. 62) with his smoking sword dripping with the blood of many foes. The battle, as recounted by the Captain, appears to be all but lost to the traitor Macdonwald and his rebel army; nevertheless, Macbeth and Banquo win the day yet again for Mother Scotland. Unlike many warriors with future occupational aspirations, Macbeth is clearly not a young man at the beginning of his military career; rather, he has had a long, seasoned record of victories and successes for his homeland. Bearing in mind the warrior culture of the clannish 11th-century Scotland, one must consider Macbeth to be the country's epic hero. His exploits are so impressive that based on the laws of Scottish tanistry (a topic to be discussed in Chapter 4), Macbeth appears to be the logical replacement for King Duncan. Even today, quite frankly, we all want to admire a character similar to the victorious Macbeth as his military prowess develops and grows into mythic status. His battlefield exploits and successes are comforting to the nonwarrior living in a warlike environment. Ironically, our first impression of the Thane of Glamis is of a leader who maintains peace for his homeland. This view, however, will forever be altered by the conclusion of Act II, scene ii of *Macbeth*.

So, why does this premise all change? Why does Macbeth choose to break his ancient warrior codes to become the usurper king? Can we not just merely lay the blame at the feet of the Weïrd Sisters or Lady Macbeth, writing off Macbeth's decisions as the callous acts of a mindless fool? Although these factors may lead Macbeth to make his devastating choices, we witness Macbeth killing Duncan by thrusting a dagger into the man that he swore to protect. Macbeth does it, not the Weïrd Sisters, not Lady Macbeth—

- ❧ *He* murders Duncan.

- ❧ *He* sends assassins to kill Banquo and Fleance.

- ❧ *He* dispatches murderers to slaughter Macduff's entire family.

No other character can take the blame for Macbeth's actions. The burning questions—how does evil come into society and why does such power overwhelm individual characters?—are right at the heart of the play (Mehl, 1983). These topics should be the foundation for classroom discussion. The very nature of a critical analysis of the play will leave you and your pupils continually searching for reasons why Macbeth makes so many self-destructive decisions leading to his nihilistic outlook at the play's conclusion. How can a patriot, with such loyalty to his country, transform into a murderous and traitorous beast?

Macbeth: A Play of Choices

Macbeth is a play of choices. Even leading up to the fateful evening at Inverness (Macbeth's castle), when he hosts his kinsman, lord, and special guest, King Duncan, Macbeth is still uncertain about which path to choose. Nevertheless, when he decides to commit his grievous act, with some assistance from Lady Macbeth, the tradition of Scotland is forever perverted and the world is thrown into nightmarish chaos. The glorious warrior accolades of Macbeth and his mythic sword that sweep through enemy troops, a staple of his battlefield successes, have now been substituted by daggers wielded with such senseless force and clumsy handling (such as leaving the murder weapons at the scene of the crime) that all positive battlefield attributes are replaced by murderous ruthlessness. As the play unfolds, and when the world of Scotland is launched into turmoil, Macbeth reverts to what he comprehends, and what is most recognizable to him—mass destruction.

Aristotle's *Poetics* and Macbeth

Herein lies the foundation of Macbeth's character and, some scholars would say, the epitome of Aristotle's tragic hero. Aristotle's term *hamartia* is very apt to the discussion of any tragic hero, but specifically to Macbeth. Hamartia is the failure or error of a character and often is mislabeled as the character's "tragic flaw." Teachers and students focus so much on the flaw of a protagonist that they fail to see the character's humanity. As Boethius points out, "One flaw is not a ruling concept" (Mangan, 1991). Aristotle's *Poetics* expresses the hero's hamartia, which often is brought about by his *hubris*, or excessive pride, leading to *peripeteia*, or a sudden reversal of fortune. At the conclusion of the tragedy, Aristotle would argue that there needs to be some moment of *anagnorisis* or recognition by the tragic hero of his faults. The tragic hero's fate arouses pity and fear, and the conclusion of the tale suggests some *catharsis* or spiritual cleansing for the character (Mangan, 1991). The character of Macbeth, however, is hard to pin down in this pre-established template set forth by Aristotle. *Macbeth* not only incorporates the themes of the medieval morality plays of the 15th and early 16th centuries, such as *Doctor Faustus*, but also integrates motifs wherein a protagonist's integrity has been tempted by a number of vices causing the hero to choose a path to either heaven or hell. Rather, the protagonist Macbeth as hero-villain, usurper and regicide, does not fit into a nice, tidy classification. He does not achieve anagnorisis nor does he ever reach a state of catharsis prior to his death. Spiritually, at the end of Act V, Macbeth is as dead as the corpse of Duncan from Act II, because he feels little remorse for his deeds. Furthermore, he reflects on life and the world, stating that life "is a tale / told by an idiot, full of sound and fury, / Signifying nothing" (V. v. 29–31); ostensibly, catharsis will never touch this man's soul. The enigmatic character of Macbeth accordingly, defies classification:

> The tradition of the drama from the days of Aristotle is that the spectator must feel moral companionship for the hero, else the tragic emotions, pity and fear, cannot affect him. The history of the stage proves that Aristotle's analysis is inadequate. To the strict follower of Aristotle [...] a tragic hero must be an enigma. No one can pity the man who loves evil for its own sake, nor can such a one cause us to fear retribution for our own acts [...] Macbeth may be a villain, and yet a good tragic hero. (Padelford, 1901, pp. 236–237)

Descending Into the Abyss of Villainy

Macbeth's humanness resonates throughout the play, in all that he does. The problem with his character, however, and the reason that actors, scholars, audiences, and readers feel very distant from him, is that by the conclusion of Act II, scene ii, King Duncan is dead and the web of lies and deceit begins to be spun. The remaining acts of *Macbeth* underscore Macbeth's villainy, not his humanity, and the paradox of his character takes root in his malicious choices and flawed decision making.

On the one hand, is it possible to examine *Macbeth*, the play and the protagonist, in the classroom and not merely dismiss this man as a murdering maniac? On the other hand, could we present his complexities as decisions enacted by a person who makes a series of bad choices? Granted, we often examine literary characters in our classrooms whose moral qualities are untenable; Macbeth, however, is an enigmatic character because of, not in spite of, his humanness, and his failings. Macbeth is not a "thinking man" akin to Hamlet. Rather, he is a doer; this characteristic has always separated him from others in battle. Unlike Hamlet, who spends five acts and one scene to respond to the ghost's plea from Act I, Macbeth is a man of action from the outset of the tragedy, even before the tragedy unfolds. Unfortunately, Macbeth's lack of thought attached to his actions is a major reason for his downfall. The very nature of Macbeth is to act first and then to think about his actions later, if at all. Do we see him as a character lamenting the killing of Macdonwald and others in the play? Certainly not. He is a trained and expert battlefield tactician and soldier.

Unlike other Shakespearean protagonists who make poor choices from the outset, Duncan and the other Scots celebrate their battle-tested hero and praise Macbeth for his victories. Even Duncan, soon to feel the murderous wrath of Macbeth, ironically bestows upon his subject the highest praise, "O valiant cousin, worthy gentleman!" (I. ii. 26). Macbeth is the warrior model, who does not expect to be named Thane of Cawdor as a reward for his loyalty. Rather, he merely protects his country and his king from rebel forces.

The Dichotomy of Human Nature and Villainy

In analyzing *Macbeth*, concentrate on the fallen world of Scotland. Unlike his other tragedies, Shakespeare provides little opportunity for the audience to understand the human nature of Macbeth. We feel the struggles of Othello as he overcomes racial prejudices and comes to terms with his own jealousy; we pity Hamlet, the young prince from Denmark whose father's murder and mother's quick remarriage leave him isolated as he is compelled to avenge his father's murder (dictated by the ghost of the same father); and we suffer with Romeo, the young Venetian, so deeply in love with the innocent Juliet, sadly barred from her presence because of the warring Montague and Capulet families. The decisions of Macbeth are so evil and utterly egregious that his very nature repels him from our own morality. As Peter Saccio (1999) states in his lecture entitled "*Macbeth*: Fair Is Foul":

> Macbeth is a bad man who is ultimately destroyed by better men, as his wife is tortured and driven to death by her own guilt. Their behavior appears to be unnatural both in the sense of being wicked and in the sense of being foreign to them. Evil is something alien and perverse.

No member of the audience can relate to the "perversity" and the very nature of evil enacted in the play. Yet, in evaluating Macbeth's character, one sees that he is not some unattainable force within each of us; rather, he is very much like us, as "alien" as his evil may be to us. What separates Macbeth from the rest of us, however, is that he crosses into the world of evil and never looks back after his initial decision to kill Duncan. He refuses to relinquish his power and becomes a dictator of fear and vengeance, an approach that clearly is the opposite of the slain King Duncan. Ironically, because Macbeth's ambition is so human, and his choices structure the basis for his villainy, the reader of this play will forever be changed. Pursuing the dichotomy of Macbeth's human nature and his villainy is the core of analysis and pedagogy of *Macbeth*, providing students with a richer and fuller classroom experience. Lastly, dissecting the human nature of the protagonist leads to a deeper understanding of the villainous underpinnings of this once heroic warrior turned monster.

The Historical Macbeth: Unraveling the Truths, Lies, and Misrepresentations

Of all the characters in literature, Macbeth ranks as one of the cruelest murderers. As written in previous chapters, his villainy is rather clear, but he requires a deeper analysis in understanding his humanity. In Shakespeare's tragedy, Macbeth's killing of the kindly King Duncan sets into motion a tumultuous and destructive pattern of treachery and bloodshed in Scotland. It is not until Macduff beheads the bloody "butcher" (V. viii. 82) that Malcolm ascends to his "rightful" role as king. Only then can order finally be restored to Scotland.

Yet, what about the real King Macbeth? Frankly, if he had read Shakespeare's play, the historical king would have sued for libel! There are so many misrepresentations and factual inaccuracies that students, and maybe even the classroom practitioner, will be shocked when they discover the true nature of the 11th-century King Macbeth. Why then does the historical figure differ so greatly from Shakespeare's fictional protagonist? There are a few reasons why the accounts vastly diverge from the true account. Before delving into a historical account of King Macbeth who ruled Scotland from 1040–1057—quite a long time for the leader of a clannish, warrior culture of 11th-century Scotland—and unlocking a valid (as far as we can surmise) accounting of his life, some historical rethinking needs to be considered. In addition, some time must be spent on the reason why Shakespeare wrote the play in the form that it exists and what issues factored into its final form.

The first and most obvious reason that the factual account was "restructured" is the presence of James I as the royal audience for the play. James I had a deep and rich understanding of the history of his homeland. Shakespeare, one of his newly appointed King's Men (formerly called the Lord Chamberlain's Men under Elizabeth I), and a working playwright and businessman, wrote for his audiences accordingly. The true account of the historical Macbeth was massaged to entertain and to play to the audiences of the Jacobean theater. Numerous volumes are filled with or dedicated to Shakespeare's awareness of his audience, but his audiences knew very little Scottish history. Because this lack of prior knowledge is an unnecessary prerequisite to an understanding of the play, Shakespeare was able to be "creative" with the historical accounts that he uncovered in his research. Shakespeare knew that tales of violence and superstition played well with Elizabethan/Jacobean audiences, and the Scottish history that Shakespeare dedicated to memory has an overabundance of each. Also, the subject matter regarding Scotland was of new interest to the English audiences in light of their newly crowned Scottish monarch. Particularly cognizant of the contemporary issues of the time, the audience of Shakespeare's England would have been pleased with the intrigue and violence regarding the monarchy in the play. To read more about the Gowrie Conspiracy and the Gunpowder Plot, two events of Shakespeare's England, see Chapter 5.

Aside from the violence and the Scottish subject matter, the running time of a production of *Macbeth* would have been relatively brief in comparison to other lengthier Shakespearean plays such as *King Lear* and *Hamlet*. *Macbeth*'s condensed length is filled with terse and shortened scenes devoid of lengthy soliloquies. Because James I liked shorter plays, the abridged writing of *Macbeth*, its production rife with witches and violence, topics that piqued the king's interest, would have suited James' limited attention span. Lastly, and less intentionally on Shakespeare's behalf, was the misrepresentation of one of the sources utilized by Shakespeare, namely Raphael Holinshed's *Chronicles of England, Scotland, and Ireland, 2nd Edition* (1587). Holinshed's *Chronicles* was a primary source that served as the backbone for the Macbeth "history," and it includes factual inaccuracies about King Macbeth of which Holinshed himself was unaware. The errors that Shakespeare reproduces were unintentional at the time of the play's composition. (All references to Holinshed reflect Hosley's 1968 edition of the work.)

How does this information pertain to a study of *Macbeth*, and how does it lend itself to classroom discussions? To teach the play in its contemporary context faithfully, the classroom practitioner needs to be able to understand the issues that surrounded the play and its creation. In doing so, one does not want to divorce Shakespeare from his art as a playwright, but rather to provide students with a fuller historical context about the play and its protagonist. Based on this historical background, classroom discussions will be more richly filled with topics and textual evidence that far surpass a pedestrian recounting of the plot. The motivation for the factors that went into the foundation of the storyline is an ongoing debate by scholars. In order to uncover the larger kernels of truth within the confusion and to further illuminate *Macbeth*, it is necessary to delve into some Scottish history. This information is very relevant to classroom study, because the history, which most certainly would have been known by James I, provides the structural framework for the play.

Defining the Royal Play

Defined by H. N. Paul (1950), a *royal play* is a high tragedy that demonstrates a picture of the mind of a noble man under emotional duress. The key idea behind a royal play is that it is written specifically for a monarch and his or her royal court. By writing for a royal audience as opposed to the diverse Globe Theater crowd, which would have been filled with individuals from all walks of life, varied intellects, and an assortment of trades, Shakespeare most likely would have postulated that those citizens in attendance at a royal play would have had a classical education and formal training in appropriate court etiquette.

Unlike his predecessor Elizabeth I, James I was not very fond of plays. He preferred outdoor activities, such as hunting, to occupy his time. Many scholars agree that Shakespeare's play was written directly for a private showing to James I and his cousin King Christian. Because James I knew the Scottish history of Macbeth and the tale of King Duff, who is discussed later in this chapter, James most likely would have been thoroughly entertained at the production. Each Jacobean subject would have been aware of the monarch's infatuation with his Scottish lineage and the pride that he took in "supposedly" tracing his ancestry to the characters of Banquo and Fleance of Shakespeare's drama; a play about James' genealogical relatives would have pleased him immensely.

Some scholars, such as Nicholas Brooke (1990), however, have disagreed with H. N. Paul's assertions that *Macbeth* was written for the private audience of James I. Brooke argued that the choice of subject in *Macbeth* had far more to do with public interest, and therefore, the public theater, than with pleasing the king: "Indeed the subject had obvious political dangers [. . .] yet, while the politics are important in *Macbeth*, they are not a royal command" (p. 76).

The Real King Macbeth

Because of the numerous incomplete and inaccurate accounts about the historical Macbeth, Shakespeare's dramatic construct has replaced the historical figure, often overshadowing the true nature of the man. "The distinction [among] the historical, mythical, and dramatic Macbeths is lost; the Macbeth of modern consciousness is invariably Shakespeare's" (Aitchison, 1999, p. 125). Consequently, a working history of Macbeth will provide a richer classroom discussion about the historical man who has become so vilified by Shakespeare's interpretation. See Chapter 9 for The "Historical" Macbeth Informational Search activity.

Mac Bethad mac Findláich, the historical Macbeth, was born circa 1005. His father, a man named Findláich, was the Mórmaer of Moray, an area located in northern Scotland. The title of mórmaer referred to a royal administrative post in 11th-century Scotland. The mórmaer, a member of the royal kin group, was an individual who oversaw the fiscal, judicial, and military issues in his respective province. Based on the responsibilities of the mórmaer, Findláich would have wielded significant power within his specific territory, as well as throughout the country of Scotland.

Lower than the mórmaers on the royal pecking order were the thanes, a group with whom the reader of *Macbeth* will be most familiar. The thane held and ruled his respective "thanage" directly and managed his territory—his royal estate—collecting revenues and taxes. Although not members of the royal kin group, these men each administered a royal estate for the king (Aitchison, 1999). Although this information pertains to the play, the title of thane did not appear until after the 12th century, and Glamis did not become a thanage until after the middle of the 13th century; therefore, Shakespeare's utilization of the Thane of Glamis, Macbeth's original title, is *anachronistic*, or befitting of another time period.

In 1020, the 15-year-old Macbeth mourned the tragic death of his father at the hands of a fellow Scot named Gillacomgain and, more than likely, Malcolm, Findláich's successor. Gillacomgain was more than a random countryman. He had ancestral bonds to the Macbeths; ironically, he was a nephew to Findláich, and a cousin to young Macbeth. After the death of Malcolm, the successor to Findláich in 1029 should have rightfully been Macbeth; as he, not Gillacomgain, had the rightful claim to the title of Mórmaer of Moray. Gillacomgain took the title instead, much to the chagrin of Macbeth: "Under the traditional system of alternating succession between collateral branches, the Mórmaership should have passed to Macbeth" (Aitchison, 1999, p. 44). In 1032, Macbeth sought revenge for the murder of his father and burned Gillacomgain and approximately 50 of Gillacomgain's allies to death. Macbeth rose to the title of Mórmaer of Moray, a title that he claimed was wrongly taken from him after the murder of his father.

To further establish his rule as Mórmaer, and some would say dominance over the deceased murderer Gillacomgain, Macbeth married Gruoch, the granddaughter of Kenneth III and the great-granddaughter of King Duff in 1033. More significantly, however, was that Gruoch was the widow of the aforementioned Gillacomgain. Although Macbeth had no children of his own, Gruoch and Gillacomgain had a son named Lulach. Macbeth eventually adopted Lulach, and after Macbeth's death in 1057, Lulach reigned as King of Scotland for a brief period (1057–1058), only to be defeated by Malcolm III in 1058. Marrying Gruoch would have had political implications for Macbeth, based on her ancestral lineage to Duff and Kenneth, "In taking Gruoch as his bride, Macbeth may be emphasizing the completeness of his victory by marrying the widow of his dead opponent" (Aitchison, 1999, p. 49). The marriage of Macbeth to Gruoch meant that Macbeth had a logical claim for the High Kingship from his father's side and now through his new wife's lineage.

The Rules of Succession: Tanistry

When reading Shakespeare and/or studying the history of monarchies, most students are aware of the traditional system of passing on inheritance and titles through the father's lineage; this system is called *primogeniture* (meaning "first born"). Although there are numerous types of ancestral rules of succession from country to country, patrilineal primogeniture states that the first, eldest male (or daughter if there are no sons) will replace the king after his death; this system is utilized in the United Kingdom. For example, in modern-day England, after the death of Queen Elizabeth II, Prince Charles will be installed as King of England. Prince Charles has two sons, Prince William of Wales and Prince Henry of Wales. William, the eldest of the two, will be named the Heir Apparent to his father if/when Charles becomes the king. After his father's death, William will be installed as king. The line of succession will, in turn, go through William's line of ancestry, and his future lineage will be the kings and/or queens of England.

Conversely, the laws in Scotland during the 11th century were quite different from today's United Kingdom. Acquiring lands and titles in Scotland was based on a system of alternating succession called *tanistry*. According to *The Oxford English Dictionary*, tanistry was "a system of life-tenure among the ancient Irish and Gaels, whereby the succession to an estate or dignity was conferred by election upon the 'eldest and worthiest' among the surviving kinsmen of the deceased lord." The individual who was the selected heir to the throne was called the *tánaise/tanist* or "appointed one," and rarely, if ever, did a son follow in his father's kingly footsteps. Two of the primary rules of the tanistry were that, first, the proposed tanist could trace his ancestry to a common royal ancestor, and, second, that the royal kin group would agree to a successor.

> Before 1040, the kingship passed not from father to son, but brother to brother. Therefore, the successor to the kingship was most likely designated during the reign of a king, to reduce tensions among branches of the royal kin group. (Aitchison, 1999, p. 11)

A modern example with an unusual twist occurred in 1999 in the Hashemite Kingdom of Jordan when King Hussein rescinded the designation of his brother, Prince Hassan, as heir to the throne, reversing the appointment from decades earlier. The king, on his deathbed, declared his son, Prince Abdullah, Crown Prince of the Hashemite Kingdom of Jordan (Jehl, 1999).

Dating back to Alpin, father of Kenneth (843–858), the kingship of Scotland in the middle of the ninth century was a single, powerful, national monarch; however, the eligibility for kingship was limited and restricted, sharing ruling responsibility among branches of the royal kin group. The tanistry system was a precarious balance between royal lineage and militaristic might. After the proposed tanist could demonstrate an ancestral tie to a great king, the royal kin, a group called the *derbfine*, would reach agreement about who the tanist would be for Scotland. This process created numerous clashes among the various Scottish clans as factions vied for the power of the High Kingship. Because of the bloody feuds that came out of the kin group's decision for the king's successor, James I of Scotland abolished the process of tanistry in the 15th century. Ironically, in composing *Macbeth,* a play that centers on the audience of James I of England/James VI of Scotland and a Stuart relative of James I of Scotland, Shakespeare examines how King Duncan breaks the pre-established rules of tanistry by naming his son Malcolm as Prince of Cumberland, a decision based on lineal primogeniture rather than the voice of the royal kin group.

The rules of tanistry prevented female succession of any kind, and it is not until Malcolm II introduced primogeniture to the Scottish royal succession for the first time in 1005, that the system of tanistry is altered. Because Malcolm II had no living sons, he feared that he would lose power based on the established rules of tanistry, because there were no other claimants to the throne through his family lineage. Malcolm II had two daughters: Doada, Macbeth's mother, and Bethoc, Macbeth's aunt and the mother of Duncan. Insisting that his grandson Duncan would be his successor, Malcolm II abandoned the tanistry system of alternating succession for primogeniture, leading to a direct line of descent through Malcolm II's royal line. This decision created a cycle of violence that ironically led to the death of Malcolm II as well as that of Duncan.

To further emphasize the differences between the tanistry system and primogeniture, notice the genealogical maps of Scotland and Macbeth in Figures 1 and 2. Lineal primogeniture would pass on in a straight line, whereas the system of tanistry has a horizontal progression. The kings and their years of reign are numbered to clarify how tanistry works. Malcolm's decision to change the pre-established tanistry system was not only self-serving, but also self-destructive.

Under Malcolm and his successors, Scotland was transformed from a Celtic clan society to a feudal society of the kind introduced in England after the Norman Conquest of 1066. In traditional Celtic society the High King had little control over the kings or chiefs he ruled; they were men of power, usually kinsmen and potential rivals, especially since royal authority was weakened by tanistry. (Harris, 2000, p. 21)

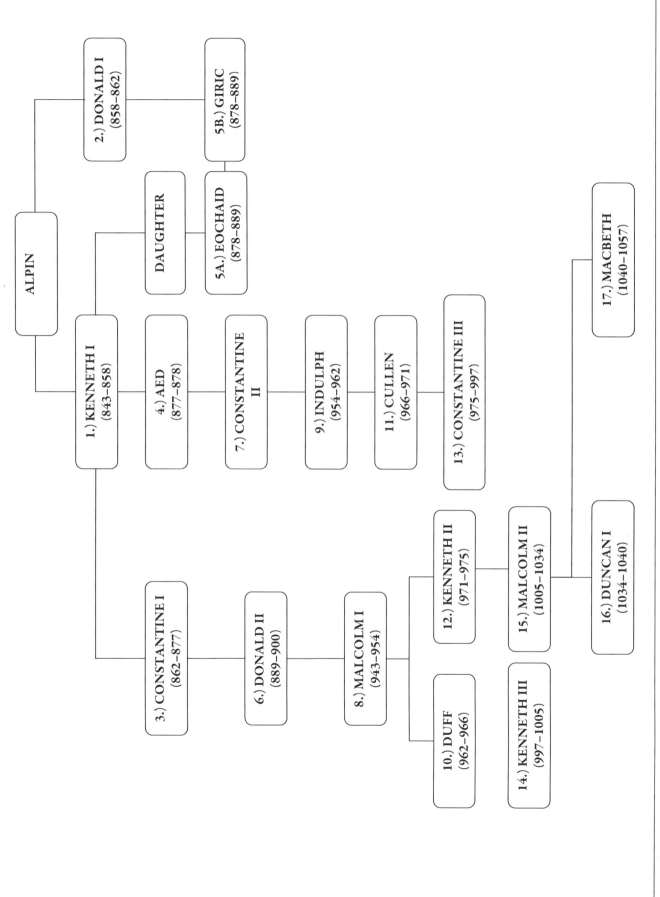

Figure 1. Genealogical map of Scottish royal lineage from 843–1057.
Note. Adapted from Aitchison (1999).

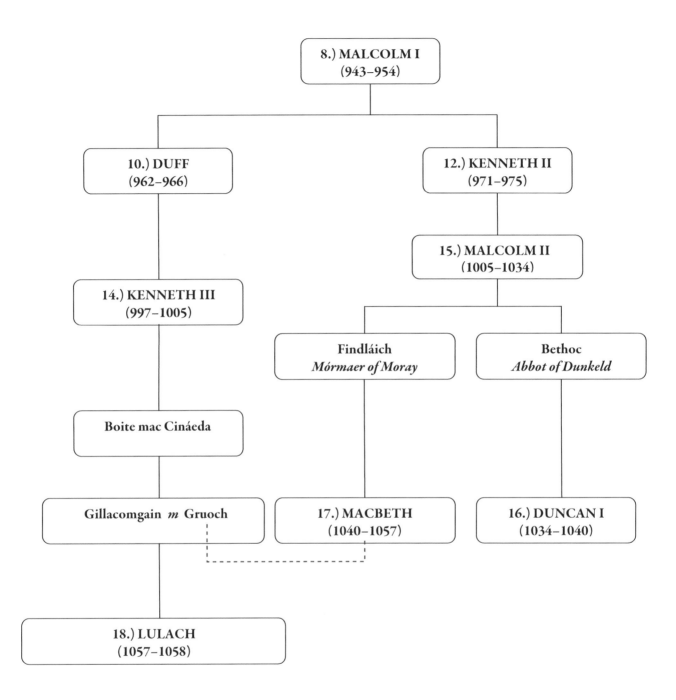

Figure 2. Genealogical map of Macbeth's lineage.

Note. This genealogical map demonstrates how the rules of tanistry, which utilized alternating succession for the role of the High King from brother to brother. Malcolm II changed the tradition in 1034. Adapted from Aitchison (1999).

King Macbeth of Alba/King of Scotland
(1040–1057)

So, how then did this historical Macbeth become King of Alba/King of Scotland? Holinshed's *Chronicles* casts some light on this subject; unlike what Shakespeare would have the reader believe in Act II of his play, the historical Macbeth does not murder Duncan in cold blood (Hosley, 1968). Rather, the warrior Macbeth killed Duncan on the battlefield of "Inverness, or (as some say) at Bothgowanan" (Hosley, 1968, p. 18), *not* at Macbeth's home castle of Inverness. Macbeth was the last ruler in the established Celtic tradition.

Macbeth was king of the Scots from 1040–1057, reigning during a transitional period in the history of Scotland. Dubbed as the "Red-King," most likely for his shocking red locks, Macbeth was a fair and just king whose intentions were "to punish all enormities and abuses which had chanced through the feeble and slothful administration of Duncan" (Hosley, 1968, p. 19). A defender of innocent people under his rule, Macbeth placed an emphasis on virtuous manners and divine service (Hosley, 1968). These kingly characteristics are attributed to Macbeth during the first 10 years of his rule as High King, marked by a pilgrimage to Rome in 1050. Upon his return, Macbeth's kingdom was still intact, quite a task in a society where bloodshed and usurpation were culturally acceptable means of survival. This detail leads us to surmise that either the citizenry was content with their king or Macbeth was more tyrannical than benevolent. After the Roman pilgrimage, Holinshed noted that there is a marked change in the man that ruled with evenhandedness (Hosley, 1968). Macbeth becomes a totalitarian despot, ruling by fear and intimidation. Was the change based on his meeting with the Weïrd Sisters years prior or something else? Herein lies the juncture in our analysis of Shakespeare's work and the history of the warrior named Macbeth.

Shakespeare's Sources

At the time Shakespeare penned *Macbeth*, England was changing, and with its new Scottish monarch James VI of Scotland/James I of England, the growing excitement for all things Scottish among the English subjects had reached a fevered pitch. Shakespeare most certainly utilized a number of primary sources in creating his "fictional" play; in particular, the basis for the majority of the story was borrowed from Holinshed's *Chronicles of England, Scotland, and Ireland, 2nd Edition* (originally published in 1587).

For Shakespeare, the work of Holinshed would be his main source; Holinshed's writing incorporated the history of Scotland from its initial beginnings to 1575.

Detailing a lengthy genealogy of the original line of kings, Holinshed's text provided an accessible primary source for the English audience.

Holinshed's *Chronicles* was a translation of the work by Hector Boece (Boethius) entitled *Scotorum Historiae* (1527). This translation has increased relevancy, specifically because of the historical inaccuracies that Boece establishes and Holinshed unknowingly upholds. Other sources that Shakespeare most certainly consulted would have been George Buchanan's *Rerum Scoticarium Historia* (1582), Reginald Scot's *Discovery of Witchcraft* (1584), and two works written by James I: *Daemonologie* (1597) and *Basilikon Doron* (1599). These last two works bear significance on the play because, as previously stated, a number of scholars agree that Shakespeare's initial production of the play may in fact have been a royal play in Hampton Court on the evening of August 7, 1606.

King Duff and Donwald (967 A.D.)

A great deal of Shakespeare's source material extracted from Holinshed's account has very little to do with the historic Macbeth or King Duncan. More than 70 years before Macbeth becomes the king of Scotland, there was a planned assassination of King Duff (966) on which Shakespeare modeled his dramatic description of Macbeth's murder of Duncan. Remember, the historical Macbeth killed Duncan on the battlefield of "Inverness, or (as some say) at Bothgowanan" (Hosley, 1968, p. 18), *not* at Macbeth's home castle of Inverness. The historical account tells us that Donwald assassinated King Duff, aided by the whispering guidance of his conniving wife, Lady Donwald, a historical predecessor to the fictional Lady Macbeth. As the history is retold by Holinshed, King Duff was suffering from an unexplained fever. During his illness, a group of witches was discovered on a wooded heath roasting a wax image of King Duff and chanting incantations over the wax duplicate of the king. King Duff's soldiers discovered the witchcraft and the king executed the witches; a few of these women were the kinfolk of Donwald. Seeking revenge for the murders, Donwald, persuaded by Lady Donwald, decided to kill King Duff. The Donwalds welcomed King Duff to their castle at Forres; surreptitiously, Donwald ordered his servants to cut King Duff's throat while he slept. The morning after the successful murder, Donwald killed the chamberlains whom he hired, blaming them for the massacre and ransacked every corner of the castle searching for the corpse of the fallen king. Notice how closely this historical account resembles the behavior exhibited by Macbeth in Act II, scene iii.

Although some of the thanes suspected Donwald of the murder, Duff's body was stealthily buried in a stream, covered with stones and gravel. Holinshed referred to the ancient Scottish superstition that blood would flow from the body when the murderer was present (Hosley, 1968). For 6 months, the weather in Scotland was a foreboding reflection of the usurpation:

> For the space of six months together, after this heinous murder thus committed, there appeared no sun by day, nor moon by night in any part of the realm; but still was the sky covered with continual clouds, and sometimes such outrageous winds arose, with lightening and tempests, that the people were in great fear of present destruction. (Hosley, 1968, p. 12)

King Duff's body was eventually recovered, and King Cullen (966–971) became his successor.

Why would Shakespeare choose to have Duncan assassinated in a similar fashion to King Duff rather than killed on the battlefield as Holinshed's text reveals? Shakespeare modeled Duncan's death after Duff's for two dramatic purposes as well as a historical consideration in light of the presence of James I. First, the staging of a battlefield scene for his production would have drastically increased the cost of the production, and, second, if this performance were indeed a royal play, then the space on stage for a full-scale battle scene would have been limited. Evidence to this hypothesis points directly to the opening scenes of the play in Act I when the action of the play resembles the epic construct *in medias res* in recounting the victorious and heroic deeds of Banquo and Macbeth in quelling the rebel army of Macdonwald and the Norwegians.

Furthermore, as a playwright, Shakespeare could add detail to the construction of his character Macbeth and focus his attentions on the interior struggles and imagination of his protagonist. For dramatic purposes the reader or viewer of the play grants Macbeth his battlefield prowess and takes the firsthand accounts of the Captain and Ross at face value. The image of Macbeth as "Bellona's bridegroom" (I. ii. 62) with "his brandished steel" (I. ii. 19) is embedded in our imaginations as audience members. When Macbeth finally decides to assassinate Duncan, Shakespeare wants the audience to witness just how far our tragic hero has fallen and how his decision is the antithesis of heroic action. By supplanting King Duncan with King Duff, the setting is a place where Shakespeare could delve into the human nature of the murdering Macbeth more readily than he could by describing the battlefield-tested Macbeth.

Lastly, as will be further discussed in Chapter 5, the murder of King Duff directly parallels the murder of James I's father, Lord Darnley, in 1567. Shakespeare's decision to include this story hearkens back to James' fear of suffering the same fate as his father. Shakespeare "probably misplaced it [the King Duff story] in this way because he wished to depict on the stage a close parallel to the Darnley murder" (Winstanley, 1970, p. 29).

Holinshed's Portrayal of Macbeth and Duncan

A primary source for Shakespeare's plot ideas, Holinshed's *Chronicles* portrays Macbeth as a man of diverse characteristics. Holinshed's Macbeth is best remembered for his exploits on the battlefield and as a ruler who treated his subjects poorly. Yet, during the first 10 years that Macbeth sat upon the throne of Scotland, he was a strong ruler, "and provided important legislation notably enhancing the central power, and also the status of women by giving [...] limited rights of inheritance to daughters and widows" (Brooke, 1990, pp. 69–70). However, to understand King Macbeth and his rise to power, consider Macbeth's ascension to power following the death of his predecessor King Duncan.

King Duncan was "so soft and gentle of nature" (Hosley, 1968, p. 14) and provided too much clemency to criminals. Historically, Macbeth was more feared than Duncan was by his fellow Scots on and off the battlefield, but one could argue that Duncan may have been the better king in terms of the qualities and characteristics that citizens look for in their monarch. Politically, Duncan's excessive "fairness" may have been viewed as a weakness by his subjects, and Macbeth would have been deemed the more appropriate leader for the warrior culture of the Scottish thanes. Duncan's reign had very few problems; yet, Holinshed points out that the thanes had become increasingly critical of Duncan's leniency in punishing miscreants, because lawbreakers in Scotland, knowing of Duncan's kindness, were habitual offenders:

> As many critics have noted, Shakespeare magnifies the criminal record of Holinshed's Macbeth and omits the exonerating circumstances, which the historian allows him. None of the tragedies so sorely tempts the reader to absent himself from sympathy with the protagonist, or even to discover in the action the didactic configuration of a belated Morality play. Yet, as the play relentlessly pursues the terrible consequences (personal, social, cosmic) of Macbeth's crimes, Shakespeare employs all the resources of his art to create in this murderer-usurper a recognizable image of ourselves. (Tromly, 1975, p. 156)

Because of Duncan's apparent ineffectiveness as a leader, the rebel Macdonwald organized a group of insurgent forces to overthrow the kingdom. Duncan's lack of decisiveness and ineptitude in quelling Macdonwald's uprising appears to be the proverbial "last straw" for the thanes, especially Macbeth and Banquo. The traitorous Macdonwald from Shakespeare's play is given a brief description, but Holinshed's account describes the rebel in much deeper detail.

Macdonwald designated himself as captain of the renegades and persuaded the Western Isle (Ireland), the Kerns, and the Gallowglasses to aid him (Hosley,

1968). Macdonwald said that Duncan was "a faint-hearted milksop more meet to govern a sort of idle monks in some cloister than to have the rule of such a valiant and hearty men of war as the Scots were" (Hosley, 1968, p. 15). King Duncan's palpable fear of Macdonwald emboldened the rebel to kill one of Duncan's top captains, named Malcolme, and smote off his head in battle. Duncan called together the thanes in a council to discuss what should be done with the traitor. Duncan's blatant uncertainty about Macdonwald and his reliance on the military advice of the king's thanes provided the thane Macbeth the opportunity to grasp the reigns of leadership and power. He and Banquo went to Macdonwald's castle to quell the uprising and neutralize the seditious threat. Before the arrival of Macbeth and Banquo, Macdonwald killed his own wife and children, and then fearing the punishment of the approaching warriors, Macbeth and Banquo, killed himself. Macbeth cut off Macdonwald's head and presented it to Duncan as proof of the traitor's death. Even though the uprising had been suppressed, Macbeth no longer viewed Duncan's softness as a characteristic that was acceptable in his 11th-century Scotland.

Unlike Duncan, Macbeth was valiant in battle but unforgiving and cruel (Hosley, 1968). In charging Macbeth and Banquo with the task of conquering Macdonwald, Duncan inadvertently shifted the power to Macbeth. Although law and order was restored to Scotland after the death of Macdonwald, a tenuous power struggle began between Duncan and Macbeth. After stopping yet another army, the Danes led by Sweno, Macbeth and Banquo encountered a group of witches before returning to Macbeth's castle. The witches inform Macbeth of the now infamous prophecy that forms the beginning of Shakespeare's dramatic interpretation:

> "All hail Macbeth, thane of Glamis" (for he had lately entered into that dignity and office by the death of his father Sinel). The second of them said; "Hail Macbeth thane of Cawdor." But the third said; "All hail Macbeth that hereafter shalt be king of Scotland [. . .] [Macbeth] shall reign indeed, but with an unlucky end; neither shall he leave any issue behind to succeed in his place. (Hosley, 1968, p. 17)

At this time, similar to Shakespeare's account, the Thane of Cawdor, because of his treasonous activities, was indicted for conspiring with Macdonwald, and, true to the predictions, Macbeth soon after is named the Thane of Cawdor. What follows for a large portion of Shakespeare's play is a narrative that duplicated the entire account of Holinshed, deviating very slightly from his *Chronicles*. However, there are a few glaring omissions and additions that need further investigation.

Textual Divergence Between Holinshed's *Chronicles* (1587) and Shakespeare's *Macbeth*

As previously stated, most of Shakespeare's plot was taken directly from Holinshed's *Chronicles*, which should be very familiar to the contemporary reader of *Macbeth*. Shakespeare recognized that his contemporary audiences were enamored with Scotland and had previously not considered Scottish history of possessing much literary value. However, Shakespeare uncovers a treasure trove of bloodshed, murder, witchcraft, deception, and treachery—fertile literary territory for a genius like Shakespeare.

Much of the plot of *Macbeth* follows Holinshed's account directly; yet, the close reader will notice a few major areas where the stories diverge. Examining the differences in the two narratives allows for a close textual study between Holinshed's history and Shakespeare's creative twists. The Donwald/King Duff assassination already has been discussed in some detail. Including this plot twist in *Macbeth* provided Shakespeare with an opportunity to develop the characters of Macbeth and Lady Macbeth in the early stages of his drama, linking the witches' prophecies to the fictional Macbeth's primary design to usurp the throne. What follows is a thorough examination into a few divergences between the two texts and key areas of the drama that lead into a further fictionalizing of the historic Macbeth. Although some are minor changes and alterations to Holinshed's text, the adjustments raise some interesting questions about Shakespeare replicating Holinshed's account verbatim, altering some areas of the *Chronicles*, and completely transforming other pieces of his text.

Banquo's Character

One reason for the changes that the reader of the play will notice involves the character of Banquo specifically. James I would have established the ancestral ties linking himself to Banquo. Shakespeare's description of Banquo and his "goodness" are a direct contradiction to Holinshed's account. Holinshed presents Banquo, the Thane of Lochaber, as a co-conspirator in the death of Duncan: "At length therefore, communicating his purposed intent with his trusty friends, amongst whom Banquo was the chiefest, upon confidence of their promised aid he slew the King of Inverness" (Hosley, 1968, p. 18). Not only does Banquo clearly know about Macbeth's plot to kill Duncan, telling no other thane, but he also does nothing to stop his countryman and friend, Macbeth. Ignoring both of these threats to the monarchy would have been a direct violation of Banquo's sworn code to his king. Why then would Shakespeare change Banquo from a character that has knowledge of the murderous plot to kill Duncan to one who is a loyal

Scotsman? Some scholars, specifically in the later stages of the Jacobean period, would lead us to believe that Shakespeare creates the character of Banquo merely to construct a foil to Macbeth.

After further analysis, however, the answer points directly to James I, the primary audience for the composition of *Macbeth*. James I was a student of his own genealogy, specifically his place in the world of Scottish kings and queens. James I had been taught, erroneously so, that Banquo was his direct ancestor in the Stuart lineage. Therefore, Shakespeare, aware of the negative reaction that this lineal mistake may have produced in his new monarch, transposed Banquo's character from a traitor to a martyr. Research into Scottish history years later uncovers the truth about Banquo, a truth that neither James I nor Shakespeare could have ever known: There is no such person named Banquo nor is there a subsequent lineage by a man named Fleance, thereby negating the witches' prophecy that Fleance's numerous children would be rulers of Scotland.

As is true of all research, sometimes "facts" can be misleading based on other inaccuracies or purposeful deceptions unknown to the researcher. Holinshed's *Chronicles* was no different, as he was misled by a work that preceded his own analysis by 50 years, Boece's *Scotorum Historiae* (1527). In examining the historical exigency for Boece's writings, one discovers that he embellished the legendary story and several incidents regarding the mythic character of Banquo, which clearly is a very un-Scottish name, to improve his stock in the eyes of his Stuart patron. As Nick Aitchison wrote in his *Macbeth: Man and Myth* (1999), "Banquo's creation was to interest and to please Boece's patron by proving an ancestor for the Stuart dynasty. Banquo was soon accepted as a genuine, historical figure, and the progenitor of the Stuart kings" (p. 118). Unlike Shakespeare, modern researchers have the ability to check and recheck the validity of information, something that Shakespeare took for granted in the 1600s.

Duncan's Death and Tanistry

The murderous plot devised by Macbeth and Lady Macbeth was really the story of Donwald's killing of King Duff. Macbeth's slaying of Duncan did not take place at Macbeth's Inverness castle, but rather on the battlefield of Enuerns near Forres, and he was installed as King of Scotland at Scone soon after:

> He [Macbeth] slew the King at Inverness, or (as some say) at Bothgowanan, in the sixth year of his reign. Then having a company about him of such as he had made privy to his enterprise, he caused himself to be proclaimed King, and forthwith went unto Scone, where (by common consent) he received the investure of the kingdom according to the accustomed manner. (Hosley, 1968, pp. 18–19)

By naming Inverness as the home of the Macbeths, Shakespeare never divulges that Inverness and Bothgowanan are both fields of battle. Therefore, this confusion of the "murder" is not an orchestrated assassination plot, but rather a very pedestrian defeat on a Scottish battlefield.

What Shakespeare also neglects to discuss in the play regarding the death of Duncan is the philosophy of the tanistry system. Frankly, why would Shakespeare bother to delve into a topic that was virtually unknown to his English audience and had been abolished more than 200 years before the first production of the play? No longer part of the traditions of Scotland, but most likely known to James I, Holinshed does not neglect to mention Macbeth's "just quarrel" or potential (and legal) pathway to the throne:

> Macbeth sore troubled herewith, for that he saw by this means his hope sore hindered (where, by the old laws of the realm, the ordinance was, that if he that should succeed were not of able age to take the charge upon himself, he that was next of blood unto him should be admitted) he began to take counsel how he might usurp the kingdom by force, having a just quarrel. (Hosley, 1968, p. 18)

Omitting this information and the manner in which Duncan was killed, while blending it into the King Duff story, embellishes the usurpation scenario and magnifies the human intensity of the drama.

The Slaughter of Macduff's Family

Murders committed in Holinshed's *Chronicles* are very commonplace and an acceptable and routine means of survival in early 11th-century life. After the death of Banquo, Holinshed and Shakespeare each fuse the historical and fictionalize the circumstances surrounding Macbeth as he slowly begins to unravel and destroy those closest to him for fear of losing power. According to Holinshed, Macbeth begins putting his noblemen to death and killing so many of his own men that thanes were hiding in fear for their lives; one such thane was Macduff, the Thane of Fife. As Holinshed recounts, Macbeth was building a very stalwart garrison on a high hill called Dunsinane Castle. He demanded that each of his thanes show up to help build the castle as a sign of unity with the High King. Macduff, fearing the apparent "team-building exercise" as a trap, neglected to attend. Although he sent workmen to aid the cause, Macduff fled to England to plead with Malcolm to claim the Scottish crown. While Macduff was away in England, Macbeth gained entrance to Macduff's castle unchallenged:

Without any resistance [. . .] Macbeth most cruelly caused the wife and children of Macduff, with all other whom he found in that castle to be slain [. . .] he confiscated the goods of Macduff, proclaiming him a traitor, and confined him out of all parts of his [Macbeth's] realm. (Hosley, 1968, p. 22)

Why Shakespeare changes this detail about Macbeth is uncertain; yet, it does lend itself to the image of Macbeth as a murdering and uncontrollable monster that many readers gravitate toward in their analysis of the play.

The Battle Against the Danes

This final item may have very little relevance to the contemporary reader/ viewer of *Macbeth*, but it provides further evidence of *Macbeth* as a royal play for the audience of James I. Holinshed clearly describes the opening battle against the Danes, not the Norwegians. There is a very pragmatic reason for this change. The royal audience of the play consisted of King James and his brother-in-law, the Danish King Christian; therefore, for political expediency and social protocol, that is, being careful not to insult the esteemed guests and familial relations of the English court, Shakespeare makes a quick editorial change in the text from Denmark to Norway, with one of the enemies being King Sweno (of Norway).

Composing *Macbeth*: Understanding the Societal Implications of the Jacobean Period

As articulated in Chapter 1, Shakespeare was certainly a playwright of his time and for all times. Needless to say, this chapter reviews some of the significant historical events that increasingly encircled numerous productions of the period, and most significantly, *Macbeth*.

James VI of Scotland/James I of England (1566–1625): The Divine Right of Kings

The history of the Stuart family line is filled with tales of murder, bloodshed, and violence. History recalls the pedantic nature of James I, while at the same time denouncing many of his policies. Although there are differing opinions about James' effectiveness as a monarch, let's be honest, Elizabeth I was a tough act to follow! The focus of this chapter is not on the reign of Elizabeth or the effectiveness/ineffectiveness of James as a monarch, but simply to point out that English life was changing with the installation of a newly crowned Scottish king.

Familial turmoil and strife filled James I's life. As a young child his mother, Mary, Queen of Scots (1542–1587), a cousin to Elizabeth I, was taken away from him and imprisoned. After James' mother, Mary, was forced to abdicate the throne of Scotland in 1567, the 1-year-old James became James VI of Scotland. In 1587, when James was 21 years old, the devoutly Catholic Mary was executed for treasonous activities based on a number of plots to assassinate the Queen, Elizabeth I. *Note:* James' mother *was not* the legendary "Bloody Mary"; this person, often confused with Mary, Queen of Scots, was Mary I (1516–1558), a member of the House of Tudor, a daughter to Henry VIII, and the Catholic half-sister of Elizabeth I.

Further evidence of James' turbulent childhood can be witnessed in the murder of his father Henry Stuart, Lord Darnley. While apparently escaping from an assassination attempt, Darnley was murdered in 1567 outside of the Hamilton's House in Kirk o' Field. James not only had to come to terms with a mother who was imprisoned during his childhood, but he also had been informed at a young age that his father was murdered; many people claimed that Mary collaborated in the murder of her husband. Scholarship varies on the validity of these claims; however, as James grew up, he suspected his mother's involvement, causing him to reject her and her Catholicism in his life. The untimely demise of each parent, naturally, had a lasting effect on James I. He lived in continuous fear of following in the tragic footsteps of his father and mother during his entire life as monarch of Scotland and England: "James I dreaded a repetition of his father's fate and the populous dreaded it for him" (Winstanley, 1970, p. 28).

Although a sense of apprehension about his safety was pervasive in the personal life of James I, as the king he espoused the theory of absolute monarchy, also known as the divine right of kings. A proponent of this philosophy, James believed that God was the only individual to whom a king should be accountable. James I was quoted as saying "A Deo rex, a rege lex," translated from the Latin as *The king is from God, the law from the king*. To further his monarchial dominance over his subjects, James penned *The Trew Law of Free Monarchies* (1598) in which he argued that a monarch is directly appointed by God and thereby does not answer to any earthly power. This view was very similar to the one held by King Henry VIII, James' great-great uncle. Established by the royal decree of Henry VIII, Elizabeth I had the constitutional power to select her successor to the throne of England. Therefore, Elizabeth named James I as her successor in 1603, and the Jacobean period transitioned, however awkwardly, from the Elizabethan Age.

The newly appointed James I actively promoted the union of the kingdoms of Scotland and England. Yet, Tudor propagandists, still loyal to Elizabeth, often would undermine the new monarchy under James, claiming that he did not understand the nature of the crown as it applied to English law:

> For five years the House of Commons debated the matter and came to the conclusion that James had misunderstood the nature of kingship. The Tudor concept of monarchy had been spelled out in the law courts of Elizabeth, and it was a concept which tells us a lot about the way in which thinkers of Shakespeare's day envisioned the relationship between a person and the office which s/he held. (Mangan, 1991, p. 22)

Witchcraft, *Daemonologie* (1597), and *Macbeth*

All historical accounts point directly to James I's interest in witchcraft and the supernatural. James played a significant role in the first Scottish witch hunts of 1590–1591, with his actions resulting in the torture and trial of approximately 100 witches, many of whom were summarily executed. At that time Scotland was replete with apparent witch reports and hundreds of citizens were burned for acts of witchery. Yet, during the trial of the North Berwick Witches, it may not have been malefic witchcraft that James sought to eradicate from Scotland but treasonous activities by sorcery that lead to direct threats to him and his wife, Anne of Denmark (Sharpe, 1999). After his marriage to Anne in 1589, when she was beset by tempests at sea, James blamed treasonous sorcery for the raising of these storms during the new queen's voyage, with witches' melting waxen images of the king, and poisoning the royal bed linens. Influenced by his father's and mother's violent deaths, James I had a grave fear of succumbing to a brutal and sudden demise. The fear that witches could be torturing him while courting the devil drove him mad.

The historical description of James I as a witch hunter akin to some sort of Dr. Abraham Van Helsing from Bram Stoker's *Dracula* is most likely an overstatement. Although his work *Daemonlogie* (1597) did become required reading for English clergymen in 1603, a great deal of his philosophical treatises reflected the contemporary view of the devil and the supernatural. James wrote *Daemonologie* to defend the anti-witch law in Scotland and to refute the account of Reginald Scot who, in his *Discovery of Witchcraft* (1584), argued that witches were not real. As a Scotsman, James clearly believed, along with other 16th- and 17th-century minds, that the devil was an actual, corporeal being. The devil constantly was tempting the soul of the individual, and the morality plays of the period reflected this struggle. View any older Warner Brothers cartoon, and you most likely will find a character struggling to make a choice, only to be tempted by an angel on one shoulder and a devil on the other. Similarly, James believed that the devil's evil power was equally as strong as the power of good. The individual must then overcome the emotions that these conflicting forces evoke within the individual. "For all its philosophical subtlety, *Daemonologie* was both an academic manifesto in favor of witch-hunting, and practical manual for the job" (Gaskill, 2005, p. 31). In 1604, James passed a law entitled "An Act Against Conjuration Witchcraft and Dealing with Evil and Wicked Spirits." This law repealed the pre-established edict by Elizabeth I, creating a much harsher punishment for the accused, serving as the law applied by the courts during a number of witchcraft trials. (Interestingly, the 1692 Salem Witch Trials in Massachusetts followed the rules established by James I in his 1604 law.) In the later stages of his life, James became increasingly skeptical about witchcraft and sorcery and would interview and debunk false claims in his Star Chamber. James Sharpe's compelling *The*

Bewitching of Anne Gunther (1999) recounts James' reputation among his contemporaries as an exploder of false accusations.

There are a number of historical connections in *Macbeth* to the biography of James I. James was the ninth Stuart monarch, a point of increased relevance in Act IV, scene i of *Macbeth* that reflects the descendents of Banquo. In 1589, James was married to Princess Anne of Denmark through a proxy marriage ceremony. Ostensibly, James sent his royal representative George Keith to stand in his stead to escort his new bride back to England. Upon leaving Denmark by sea to be united with her new husband, the queen's ship was beset by a series of storms. Anne's ship was supposed to sail from Denmark to Scotland, but thunder, lightning, and rain forced the ship to seek refuge in Oslo. James believed that the storm was a result of diabolical planning and accused witches for causing the storm (Greenblatt, 2004). Shakespeare knowingly included one of the "withered" hags in Act I, scene iii. speaking angrily about a "rump-fed runnion" (I. iii. 7), whose rudeness causes her to seek revenge against a sailor, the woman's husband, by means of a storm at sea. The witch promises that she will sail in a "sieve" or a boat, "But in a sieve I'll thither sail, /And, like a rat without a tail, / I'll do, I'll do, and I'll do" (I. iii. 9–11). This quotation reflects the Jacobean belief that witches sought revenge for perceived slights against them.

Clearly, Shakespeare would have spent a great deal of time reading *Daemonologie*. "The important thing about the influence of James' *Daemonologie* upon Shakespeare's *Macbeth* is that James' literal belief in—and obsessions with—the powers of darkness made available to Shakespeare a vocabulary for talking about these energies" (Mangan, 1991, p. 106). However, as we have discussed in the previous chapter, Holinshed utilized the term "Weïrd Sisters" and referenced sorcerers, not witches, in his *Chronicles*. Therefore, in order for Shakespeare to make a clearer connection with the royal audience of James I, he included witches/witchcraft as a central focal point in Act I, scene i of *Macbeth*. The "fair and foul" setting in Act I may have resulted from the equinoctial storms (occurring in March 1606), which caused a gloomy atmosphere throughout London.

The increasingly dreary weather would have negatively affected the psyche of the Jacobean populous. Shakespeare's *Macbeth*, with its ominous themes of usurpation, murder, betrayal, and sleepwalking, would have found fertile ground in the minds of his royal patrons. "According to James, one of the two great passions that led men into temptation, that made them fit subjects for the Devil's Work, was ambition" (Campbell, 1968, p. 214).

Basilikon Doron (1599)

Another work by James I was *Basilikon Doron* (1599). The title of the work, which translates as "royal gift," was written as a private letter to James I's 4-year-old son, Henry Frederick Stuart, Prince of Wales. The text outlines instructions to Henry on how to be an effective king who rules over his subjects with a moral compass. The book is divided into three sections: The first section illustrates a king's responsibility to his personal spirituality through Christianity; the second section delineates the responsibility of kingship, specifically in dealing with his subjects; and the third section describes the everyday "kingly" behaviors that demonstrate how a good king should live each day. The *Basilikon Doron* presents the theme of absolute monarchy and the divine right of kings, while at the same time extolling the goodness of the king. "In *Basilikon Doron*, James recognized the inevitable conflict between private and public morality, as well as the necessity for political expediency" (Brooke, 1990, p. 75).

The Gowrie Conspiracy (August 5, 1600)

James I often dealt with threats of violence and assassination during his reign as king in Scotland and England. In August 1600, while he was still James VI of Scotland, James survived a plot to usurp his throne. Although the "facts" of the Gowrie Conspiracy are still murky, the essentials details of the conspiracy are as follows: The third earl of Gowrie, a 22-year-old man named John Ruthven and his 19-year-old brother Alexander Ruthven welcomed James to the Gowrie House, claiming that there was a man whom Alexander had encountered on the previous evening who was concealing a pot filled with gold pieces. Alexander requested that James accompany him to the house, because Alexander was fearful that because the gold was of foreign currency, it could be seized by the magistrate. Therefore, James, in the company of the Duke of Lennox and other courtiers, followed Alexander to the Gowrie House. According to the story reiterated by James time and again, he claimed that he was imprisoned by the Gowrie brothers with threats of physical violence and assassination. While a "prisoner" at the Gowrie House, James was rescued by his courtiers, and both of the young Gowrie men were killed. Jacobean supporters praised the escape of their king, while detractors claimed that James was involved in the conspiracy and wanted to eradicate political competitors. There was a dramatic version of the Gowrie Conspiracy entitled *Gowrie* that the King's Players rehearsed a few times during November 1604, but it was feared that the production ventured into dangerous grounds and so it was never played at court (Paul, 1950). As a player in the court, Shakespeare would have been cognizant of the assassination attempt on James and weaved the theme of distrust into the fabric of his drama, specifically the breach of the hospitality codes and "double trust" mentioned in Chapter 2.

Anti-Catholic Sentiments in Elizabethan and Jacobean England

Whether Shakespeare was a practicing Catholic is unclear; however, what is obvious from biographical accounts of his childhood is that he was indoctrinated into Catholicism. The ongoing rift between the Protestants and Catholics in England arose from theological approaches and the differences in their spirituality.

Sixteenth-century Catholics believed there needed to exist "a rigid structure of spiritual authority, whereby God's mysteries could be explained to them" (Mangan, 1991, p. 9). Therefore, Catholics relied on papal authority, historically handed down from Saint Peter, the first pope, to serve in the role of the spiritual mediator between God and Catholic laymen and women. On the one hand, the priesthood was structured to provide a clear hierarchal chain from the pope directly to Catholics. On the other hand, Protestants held the belief that a minister, who was respected among the congregation, would serve not as a mediator, but as a pastor. "Men and women approach God and partake of his holiness not by virtue of a mediating priest or hierarchy or authority, but through one's own personal and individual faith" (Mangan, 1991, p. 10). Aside from differing theological interpretations, these distinct views on worship were the crux of the Jacobean theology in 16th- and 17th-century English life.

During Elizabeth's reign, there was speculation that Roman Catholics were siding with Spain to assassinate Elizabeth I, thereby returning England to a Catholic state.

Although Catholicism was illegal under Elizabeth I's reign, Elizabethan Catholics would avoid persecution if they conducted themselves in an appropriate manner, worshiped rather infrequently, and remained fully loyal to her crown. Every member of Parliament had to swear the Oath of Supremacy that acknowledged Elizabeth as the head of the Church of England and rejected papal authority.

Now, under Jacobean rule, Catholics felt the zeal and hatred of Protestant England. In Antonia Fraser's (1996) examination of the Gunpowder Plot and its historical underpinnings entitled *Faith and Treason: The Story of the Gunpowder Plot*, she cites the imprisoned Jesuit Superior William Weston who stated in 1603, 2 years prior to the Gunpowder Plot, "Catholics now saw their own country, the country of their birth, turned into a ruthless and unmoving land. The Protestants lay in ambush for the Catholics, betrayed the Catholics, attacked the Catholics with violence and without warning" (p. 22).

"Remember, Remember the 5th of November": The Gunpowder Plot (1605)

By the spring of 1605, a group of Catholic radicals, disgusted by the institutional prejudice, decided to take matters into their own hands. By today's standards they would be labeled as terrorists.

Although early 17th-century English subjects would have been made aware of the Gowrie Conspiracy and their monarch's swashbuckling escape from peril, more Englishmen and women would have directly experienced the Gunpowder Plot of 1605. Even today, the name of Guy Fawkes, one of the conspirators of the Gunpowder Plot, is still remembered on November 5 at an annual national holiday celebration in the United Kingdom as well as in other former British colonies. Now called Guy Fawkes Night or Bonfire Night, effigies of "guys" (sold for "a penny for a guy") are burned as the skies are illuminated with fireworks and bonfires fueled by "guy" effigies. Westminster Palace still is searched annually prior to the State Opening of Parliament in October/November by the Yeoman of the Guard, the monarchy's Secret Service, as a ceremonial remembrance of the failed plot.

When Shakespeare wrote *Macbeth* in 1606, "the Gunpowder Plot of 1605" or "the Powder Treason" as Shakespeare's contemporaries would have called the nearly successful act of terrorism, was a reaction to the growing anti-Catholic sentiment that surrounded England at that time. The plot comprised 13 pro-Catholic conspirators lead by Robert Catesby and aided by munitions expert Guy Fawkes. This clandestine coterie wanted to eradicate James I and the Houses of Lords and Commons as they convened in November for the State Opening of Parliament. Placing 30 kegs of gunpowder in the basement of the House of Lords in the Palace of Westminster during the State Opening of Parliament, the plotters dug a tunnel from a house that stood next to Parliament and positioned the kegs directly below where the meeting was to be held. The gunpowder was discovered before the plan could reach fruition, and many of the conspirators were caught and publicly executed. (Students may be familiar with the 2005 film *V for Vendetta*, which describes a vigilante who successfully destroys the totalitarian state of a futuristic Great Britain by reenacting the Gunpowder Plot.)

Aside from the plotters directly involved in the conspiracy, another man, Reverend Henry Garnet, S.J., a Jesuit priest and the Jesuit superior of England, was hanged on May 13, 1606, for his foreknowledge of the plot. The Jesuits were the symbol of Roman Catholicism in Jacobean England, and their involvement in such activities would have raised a great deal of suspicion by James I and his Secretary of State and chief of ministry Robert Cecil. The Jesuits were viewed as treasonous and seditious priests in England, whose primary goal, according to Elizabethan and Jacobean supporters, was to overthrow the Protestant monarchy and to create a Catholic state. In order to establish more stability with the anti-Catholic sentiment that was flourishing in England at the time, new Recusancy Acts were passed on February 22, 1604, ordering all Catholic priests, especially the Jesuits, to leave England. Instead of creating harmony and union, the Recusancy Acts split the country even further apart (Nostbakken, 1997).

A Jesuit colleague, Reverend Oswald Tesimond, S.J., heard the confession of Catesby, who informed the priest of the plotters' plans. Tesimond, uncertain about what to do with this foreknowledge of treasonous activity, asked Catesby to release the priest from the sacramental seal and seek the advice of an interpreter, in this case, his Jesuit brother and superior Garnet. All Catholic priests, after hearing an individual's confession, may not reveal any detail of a penitent's sinful admissions. However, if the absolving priest needs support or clarification about a specific sinful act, then he may seek the counsel of a more experienced cleric to act as an interpreter. In this specific case Tesimond conferred with Garnet.

Although the idea of what can and cannot be kept secret seems confusing, according to *The Catholic Encyclopedia*, the seal of the confessional is clear:

> As Canon 21 of the Fourth Lateran Council (1215), binding on the whole Church, lays down the obligation of secrecy in the following words: "Let the priest absolutely beware that he does not by word or sign or by any manner whatever in any way betray the sinner: but if he should happen to need wiser counsel let him cautiously seek the same without any mention of person. For whoever shall dare to reveal a sin disclosed to him in the tribunal of penance we decree that he shall be not only deposed from the priestly office but that he shall also be sent into the confinement of a monastery to do perpetual penance. (Nolan, 1913, p. 649)

As the interpreter to his Jesuit brother, Garnet now held the knowledge of the plot and with it, very powerful and potential treasonous information. Remember, Spain did want England to return to a Catholic state prior to the defeat of the Spanish Armada in 1588, and if such a plot were to reach fruition, it would have potentially allowed the Catholics to gain control of the English monarchy. Yet, scholarship is unclear about how much of the plot Garnet truly knew, and what, if any, personal involvement Garnet actually had in seeing the plan come to fruition.

In the case of Tesimond and Garnet, if such a confession were to have happened today, neither priest would be held responsible for the actions of the confessor. For example, if, prior to the terrorist attacks on September 11, 2001, one of the terrorists went to confession and informed a priest of the plan to attack the World Trade Center and the Pentagon, the Seal of the Confessional would not apply because there would be no sin that had been committed, and therefore, no need for absolution. Confession about a future sinful act does not qualify for forgiveness.

After the Gunpowder Plot

Jacobean England was buzzing with the growing information of the conspiracy to assassinate the monarch; therefore, a great many rumors and false details were spread across England. Initially, the attempt to murder James hearkened back to the murder of James' father and played into James' increasing apprehension about his own mortality: "The Gunpowder Plot was compared by James himself to a very similar plot against his father; i.e. the Darnley murder, and hence both Shakespeare himself and his audience had been recently and painfully reminded of the Darnley murder" (Winstanley, 1970, p. 28). Needless to say, the reaction of the citizenry reached a fever pitch regarding anti-Catholic sentiment, and an already volatile situation had become even more intense.

After the plot was uncovered, James I declared that he had a premonition about the conspiracy, claiming that it was the work of the devil: "The Privy Council of Scotland believed that the Gunpowder Plot itself was planned by evil spirits of Scotland (directly inspired by Satan), and wrote James a congratulatory letter on his escape from the said Satanic Plot" (Winstanley, 1970, p. 30). Historians tend to agree on the fact that James' reason for blaming the conspiracy on the devil would have lessened anti-Catholic tensions that were once again ignited in England. James did, however, pass an act of Parliament that attempted to control Catholics. As Michael Wood states in his very thorough biographical account entitled *Shakespeare* (2003):

> An act of Parliament was now passed mentioning particularly those 'who adhere in their hearts to the popish religion' but 'do nevertheless the better to hide their false hearts repair sometimes to the church to escape the penalty of law.' Everyone now had to receive [Protestant] Holy Communion at least once a year, or pay a huge £20 fine in the first year, 40 in the second and 60 in each succeeding year. Local constables had to give the justices of the peace the names of all papists absent from communion. (p. 290)

The names of the conspirators were plastered across England and many of these names would have been familiar to the Shakespeare family in his hometown of Stratford. Based on his relationship with his patron, the Earl of Southampton, Shakespeare most certainly would have, at the very least, known of the conspirators because they were from similar social strata. Ironically, Shakespeare's daughter, Susanna, was on a list of 21 people summoned to the Stratford church court in May 1606 for not receiving Easter communion on April 20, 1606 (Wood, 2003).

Equivocation: Saying Nothing
and Everything at Once

Before his death, Father Garnet wrote "A Treatise of Equivocation," which instructed Catholics how to evade telling the truth, yet not having to lie to Protestants who would ask them specific points about their faith, thereby avoiding the sin of lying under oath. According to Antonia Fraser (1996), "the underlying principle of equivocation was that the speaker's words were capable of being taken in two ways. Only one of which was true" (p. 242). In *Macbeth*, the porter jokes about the term equivocation, and contemporaries of Garnet claimed that "he would be hanged without equivocation for all his shifting and faltering" (Fraser, 1996, p. 282). Scholars of *Macbeth* often comment that the play is filled with a number of equivocations that neither provides a positive nor a negative response. One such example is in the beginning of Act II, scene iii, when, prior to opening the door to Macduff and Lennox, the porter makes many overt and veiled references to the recently executed Garnet. Obvious references to Garnet and the failed "Powder Plot" among Jacobean audiences would have bolstered their support of James due in large part to his swift and immediate termination of the threat by the Catholics. The classroom practitioner may want to examine the ostensibly comic speech of the porter and connect his words and ideas to the societal context of the Jacobean audience.

Drama in the Classroom and on Stage

One maxim regarding the study of Shakespeare every English teacher should keep in mind is "Shakespeare should be seen and not read." Many of us have had college professors who voiced this thought. The quotation was usually followed with a fact check that the hoi polloi in the Elizabethan/Jacobean eras watched Shakespeare's plays, cheering the hero, booing the villain, laughing at the fool, and empathizing with the wayward protagonist without reading any of the Bard's folios. All of this drama and comedy occurred, we presume, with audience understanding of plot, awareness of character, comprehension of conflict, and appreciation of the imagery and puns evoked by the actors soliloquizing on stage. How did this illiterate crowd, these groundlings, seem to "get it," while many of our students do not?

With this information preceding my entrance into the classroom a few decades ago, I resolved that to learn Shakespeare well, one must act out the scenes. So Shakespearean study in my classroom, like all drama, means that students will be out of their seats, text in hand, portraying characters. Like the plays I direct on stage, movement and speaking contribute to comprehension. Sitting in an uncomfortable desk, period after period, does not help muscle memory. Joining reading with the kinesthetic does improve comprehension—so do funny hats, silly voices, and bad accents.

Teaching *Macbeth* requires educators to approach the play as dramatic text, not literary text. This method recognizes that different comprehension lenses apply to different reading experiences. As a work of tragedy, *Macbeth* needs expression, that is, student reaction in the present tense, with student review of the text later. The richness of Shakespeare's language should evoke the auditory and the visual senses. This merging of the senses will augment comprehension. Student questions occur at the point of confusion, which then gets clarified in the reader response and class discussion process. Students are reading in a way that is similar to listening to an audiobook on an iPod or in the car. The difference is that simulating a dramatic experience combines a few factors. First, students are getting up in front of the class and acting (or trying to). The rest of the class follows the words on the page and, at the same time, listens to their classmates.

You may want to vary the experience at times:

- Have the class members just listen to their classmates act out a scene. Teacher participation is helpful because we know the play and are more familiar with the language.

- Pause in the middle of a scene at a particular passage and discuss its meaning.

- Have the students take reader response notes, which I favor, on what they read. This process helps the educator get a sense of class comprehension.

- Have students create an essay question on a particular passage. You may want the student to answer it or exchange questions and have the class respond. The point of the reading approach is to help students make meaning of what they read.

This chapter provides activities that incorporate drama in the classroom, and information and suggestions for producing a full-scale performance of *Macbeth* in your school.

Costumes and Props

Depending on your time and budget, consider costuming the characters. Students with an eye for fashion design may enjoy creating costumes for characters. This idea may range from a pencil sketch to a more ambitious actual costume. Again, each class is unique and different skills and talents occur in a group from year to year. Sometimes a simple fast food crown may serve as Duncan's and, eventually, Macbeth's kingly costume.

Plastic swords and daggers help increase student participation. A bell is useful, too. Again, students who are getting out of their seats and carrying a sword or other props when reading Shakespeare create a whole-body experience that incorporates listening, speaking, reading, and writing, the cornerstones of language arts.

Getting Started in the Classroom

To establish a metacognitive approach to thinking about reading the play, hand out Act I, scene i. Applying a critical reading process, as noted below, for the opening scene immediately sets the tone about how the play will be read for meaning.

- Invite three student volunteers to play each witch.

- Place silly hats on their heads.

- Appoint a special effects person to simulate "lightning" by flicking the lights on and off. The rest of the class creates "thunder" for a few seconds by stomping its feet. (Yes, the class and teacher below do wonder if the ceiling is about to crash, but someone must suffer for art.)

- Make sure the actors speak in "witchy" voices. Of course students will laugh, and the approach is silly, but consider how positive the tone and atmosphere in the classroom will be at the beginning of the *Macbeth* unit.

- Use the "Open Up the Keeley Doors" handout with this activity (see Chapter 8, Handout 12). Copy the scene text in the middle of the diagram and follow the activity's directions. You may choose to do this first and act out the scene second or act out the scene first and then have the students annotate their responses.

- Discuss the "fair is foul and foul is fair" line. Note how the words relate to the outcome of the war and the weather.

- Observe the witches' reference to their "familiars." Some students may compare the familiars to the "daemons" in the book or film version of Philip Pullman's *The Golden Compass*.

- Assign students to create their own "familiar." They should speak about the reasons for their choice.

The following sections break the play into acts, providing multiple objectives and different dramatic activities that can be used in the classroom to fulfill each objective.

Classroom Objectives: Act I–Act V

Act I

Objective: To distinguish between two character types and comprehend how language informs the reader/listener about characterization in Act I, scene iii.

- Read the scene aloud, observing particularly how Macbeth and Banquo react to the witches' prophecies.

- Consider a modern language rewrite of Macbeth's and Banquo's reactions to Ross and Angus' news from the king. These lines can be performed aloud and usually receive great response from classmates. Work in cooperative learning groups, giving each planning time and up to 2 minutes of presentation time.

- Highlight Act I, scene iii, lines 134–138. Review Banquo's response and advice to Macbeth about trusting the "instruments of darkness." Assess the effectiveness of peer pressure on teenage and adult behavior in positive and negative ways. What do Banquo's remarks say about his viewpoint? A debate can help students explain their points of view about peer pressure.

- Select a quotation from a prominent person in the newspaper—explain the character's intention. Provide background detail and make a prediction about future responses. If relevant, look at the connotative and denotative meaning behind the words and phrases quoted by the speaker.

Objective: To infer interior and exterior meaning through the dramatization of Lady Macbeth in Act I, scene v.

- Featuring Lady Macbeth, this scene contains one of the great female soliloquies in drama. Have your class consider her facial expression by manipulating their own expressions as she reads the letter from her husband aloud and then comments on the news contained in the missive.

- Observe how Macbeth's letter never reveals that Banquo was with him. How does this "misinformation" influence Lady Macbeth's reaction to the letter? Form small groups and discuss her reaction. Create a fictional follow-up speech for Lady Macbeth that is based on Macbeth's actual acknowledgment of Banquo's presence. Would Lady Macbeth have responded differently had she known that Banquo was present?

- In acting this scene keep in mind that Lady Macbeth has not seen her husband for months. She says "Hie thee hither," or hurry home. After reading the letter she cannot stop thinking that her husband is going to be king. This thought echoes and rebounds in her brain. Reinforce this point by having the students hear Lady Macbeth jumping for joy internally with "my husband's going to be king" again and again.

- When the messenger interrupts her thoughts with "The King comes here tonight" (I. v. 35), she is so immersed in her fantasy of her husband as king, that she takes the messenger's remark as a wish fulfilled. Her response, "Thou 'rt mad to say it" (I. v. 36) reveals an incorrect interpretation of a literal sentence. There should be a pause after her response, followed by mental clarification and body language that the messenger actually means Duncan.

Objective: To review the influence of peer pressure through the interaction between Lady Macbeth and Macbeth in Act I, scenes v and vii.

- When greeting her husband, Lady Macbeth begins with a reference to his letter and makes her plan for Duncan's demise immediately clear. Her husband announces that the king will be arriving and leaving "as he purposes" (I. v. 70). Later, Macbeth says, "We will speak further" (I. v. 83). He is more nonchalant about the witches' prophecy than his wife. Depending on your time, divide the class in pairs and have them briefly interpret the exchange between the two characters. Ask for a few volunteers to act out their interpretation, keeping peer pressure in the forefront of their acting.

- Have some groups select a section of scene v, while others present a portion of scene vi to dramatize in front of the class.

Act II

Objective: To comprehend the dagger speech as an early example of Macbeth's struggle to avoid temptation.

- Read through the dagger soliloquy. Discuss whether students, as directors of the play, would show the audience a floating dagger or not. Consider how each directorial decision would enhance or diminish this scene. For example, I chose not to show the dagger when I directed the play for a high school performance, because the language and the movement were sufficient for audience comprehension.

- The dagger scene visualizes the appearance/reality motif in this play, revealing specifically how Macbeth's inability to distinguish one from the other bodes poorly for his future success.

Objective: To study the rhythm of iambic pentameter in the murder scene in Act II, scene ii.

- Have your actors read the quick exchange between Macbeth and Lady Macbeth after Macbeth enters (line 19). Note the question and answer pattern. The rapid interaction heightens the scene's tension, continuing Macbeth's sense of uncertainty even after the murder has been committed.

- Students also should be introduced to iambic pentameter here. An iamb has a short-long syllable pattern. An effective way to teach students how to find iambic pentameter is to read through the lines with them, having them "drum" the beats with their hands. You can have them pat out the beats on their legs or clap together as they read the lines to mark the rhythmic pattern.

Objective: To look at the porter scene as thematic microcosm or comic relief in Act II, scene iii.

- Dramatically read the porter scene, involving the class or a few students in the knocking sequence. Have someone overact the porter's soliloquy from the view of an overly tired, groggy drunk who has been awakened early in the morning.

- Now, read the scene with the approach that reinforces the setting, Macbeth's castle, as a place that resembles hell. Portray the porter as the gateway greeter for the devil.

- Discuss with the class which of the two aforementioned approaches best suits the action.

Objective: To review theme, understatement, foreshadowing, irony, and characterization in the text in Act II, scene iii.

- In this scene Lennox's speech functions thematically as an example of the Elizabethan/Jacobean view of order in the universe. They believed that the king represented God on Earth; therefore, Duncan's unnatural death would have ramifications beyond himself. The foundation has been overturned and balance must be reestablished. Consider sound effects here or get the class actor to demonstrate each image in Act II, scene iii, lines 61–69.

- Macbeth's response is understatement in Act II, scene iii, line 70.

- Dramatize the scene with many students participating. Consider all of the roles. Lady Macbeth's remark, "hideous trumpet calls to parley" in Act II, scene iii, line 94, foreshadows warring factions on a battlefield.

- Macbeth's speech, Act II, scene iii, lines 107–112 aptly and ironically tells the truth about his "blessèd time."

- Macbeth's poetic description of Duncan's death contrasts with Macduff's blunt detail in Act II, scene iii, line 117.

- After dramatizing the scene, have the students analyze each section, noting the responses of the characters. Consider Malcolm and Donalbain's decision to flee. Depict the aftermath of Duncan's sons' decision in a gos-

sipy party situation. One party could be with the Macbeths in attendance;
the other could involve those who think like Macduff.

Act III

Objective: To analyze Macbeth's character and Shakespeare's use of irony through
the "To be thus is nothing" soliloquy in Act III, scene i, lines 52–77.

- After reading Macbeth's soliloquy aloud, hand out a copy of the speech
  for student analysis. Apply the "Open Up the Keeley Doors" activity
  (Handout 12, p. 131) with predicting, clarifying, questioning, and summarizing tasks. After reviewing the imagery and questions about the language, debate a current events issue that involves freedom vs. security.
  What are the consequences of emphasizing one over the other?

- Consider the irony of Macbeth complaining about a world where he is
  powerful, but does not feel safe. Note the imagery of a "fruitless crown"
  (III. i. 66).

Objective: To compose a creative behind-the-scene dialogue evoking character
motivation and demonstrating awareness of plot in Act III, scene i.

- Compose and dramatize a scene that depicts the two murderers waiting at
  an inn before meeting with King Macbeth. Consider what the characters
  might say and their reasons. What concerns would they have?

- Divide the class into random groups with one group creating a serious
  drama, another constructing a comedy, one group writing in teen-speak,
  and still another composing dialogue in couplets to rewrite this scene.

Objective: To study the function of dramatic motif and to analyze the relationship between Macbeth and Lady Macbeth in Act III, scenes ii–iv. You may want
to complete all of these activities, select a few, or allow the students to choose
which of the following activities they would like to complete as individual or
group projects.

- Develop 10 additional ways to say "Be innocent of the knowledge, dearest chuck" (III. ii. 51). Each one should evoke the aura of caring while
  maintaining a secret.

- Create a podcast evoking the "critter and varmint" images in Act III, scene
  ii. Include snakes, scorpions, bats, beetles, and crows. Incorporate these
  creatures in a sound-based radio program that reflects the growing isola-
  tion between Macbeth and Lady Macbeth. Tips for creating podcasts for

the classroom can be found at http://learninginhand.com/podcasting/create.html.

- Dramatize another scenario where there is an appearance/reality theme, such as portraying the Macbeths planning the banquet.

- Create a silent film depicting the difficulty the Macbeths are having falling asleep. Add sound effects but avoid spoken dialogue.

- Construct a history of the Third Murderer. Who is he and how did he end up working for Macbeth?

- Place the Banquo ghost scene in a different context, such as a corporate board meeting, a school board meeting, a classroom situation, or a family holiday dinner. Create a troubled protagonist who is the only person able to see a ghost. Use the Banquo ghost scene as a model and compose dialogue for your ghost in iambic pentameter or couplets.

- Determine which songs would be on the following characters' iPod, and explain the reasons for your choices:

  - Macbeth

  - Lady Macbeth

  - Macduff

  - Malcolm

Objective: To reinforce the function of the Greek chorus and to understand Lennox's role in the play in Act III, scene vi.

- Assign the "Open Up the Keeley Doors" activity (Handout 12, p. 131) with Lennox's speech (III. vi. 1–27). After reading this scene aloud, consider its importance in regard to plot. Why is this conversation between Lennox and another Scottish Lord, who is probably Angus, important to the storyline?

- What is the function of a Greek chorus? Compare Lennox's remarks to that of the chorus in Sophocles' *Oedipus* or *Antigone*. Select a current event in the news and debate the topic, using a chorus in the same way Sophocles, Aeschylus, or Euripides would.

Act IV

Objective: To encourage a multiple intelligence interpretation of the witches' brew in Act IV, scene i. Observe the ingredients thrown into the cauldron. The scene combines the comical with the horrible.

✀ Create an actual or theoretical recipe to match the witches' brew. Turn your classroom into the "Kitchen of Horrors" as individuals or groups present their special ingredients. There, undoubtedly, will be active class participation. Have the students keep in mind the reason for the witches' cauldron activity; otherwise, you have an activity that is interesting for its own sake, but not really related to the play's meaning.

✀ Hecate enters with a compliment to the three witches. Because they all sing "Black Spirits," a song from Middleton's *The Witches*, scholars believe that her lines were interpolated (Mowat & Werstine, 2004). See the sample song lyrics below:

> Black spirits and white,
> Red Spirits and gray,
> Mingle, mingle, mingle,
> You that mingle may!
> Tiffin, Tiffin, keep it stiff in;
> Fire drake, Puckey, make it lucky;
> Lyer Robin, you must bob in.
> A round, a round, about, about
> All ill come running in, all good keep out!
> (Hazleton, 1925, p. 633)

✀ After reading this scene, review all of the interactions between Macbeth and the witches. Comment on how he relates to them and how they relate to him. For example, in this scene, the second witch says, "Something wicked this way comes" (IV. i. 45).

✀ The scene closes with Macbeth resolved to kill Macduff and everyone associated with the Thane of Fife. How do Macbeth's words inform the reader about his character?

Objective: To review the Macduff family murder sequence in terms of plot, character, and conflict in Act IV, scene ii. Choose from the following activities or allow students to complete one individually.

✀ Have students create a musical collage of songs that warns Lady Macduff in a manner similar to Ross and the messenger's pleading. They should play the collage for the class, explaining their choices.

✀ Who is the messenger in this scene? Have students review all of the possibilities and present a theory in a speech or PowerPoint presentation .

✀ Macduff leaves his family unprotected in his quest to seek military support from Malcolm. Allow students to support or denounce his decision to leave in a news show segment, in a manner similar to political punditry seen on television.

Objective: To discuss qualities of leadership by reviewing the behavior of Malcolm and Macduff. Literary terms reinforced are point of view, dramatic irony, personification, and imagery in Act IV, scene iii.

- In acting out this scene in class, take the speeches in segments. The action is minimal because both characters sit and talk.

- Consider Malcolm's point of view. What does he say to indicate caution and wariness? See Act IV, scene iii, lines 15–20.

- Twice in this scene Malcolm compares himself to a lamb. What does this image suggest about his leadership? (See IV. iii. 19 and IV. iii. 65.)

- Macduff says, "Each new morn / New widows howl, new orphans cry" (IV. iii. 5–6). These lines offer an opportunity to review dramatic irony with the students.

- Personification examples abound in this scene: "new sorrows / Strike heaven on the face" (IV. iii. 6–7); "Bleed, bleed, poor country! / Great tyranny, lay thou thy basis sure, / For goodness dare not check thee. / Wear thou thy wrongs" (IV. iii. 39–42), and "I think our country sinks beneath the yoke. / It weeps, it bleeds, and each new day a gash / Is added to her wounds" (IV. iii. 49–51). Have the students locate examples of personification in the newspaper and/or create some examples of their own.

- Macduff's loyalty test: List the sins that Malcolm enumerates, explaining the reasons why he would be a poor replacement for Macbeth. Analyze the response Macduff gives for each.

- Malcolm lists the kingly graces that he lacks in Act IV, scene iii, lines 107–110. Macduff's response, self-banishment from Scotland, convinces Malcolm that Macduff is a true patriot.

- Discuss patriotism. What behaviors distinguish a patriot in our country?

- Class discussion or essay opportunity: Review the following quotations about patriotism (Moncur, 2007). Select one and discuss.

    - "'My country, right or wrong,' is a thing that no patriot would think of saying except in a desperate case. It is like saying, 'My mother, drunk or sober.'"—G. K. Chesterton (1874–1936)

    - "It is not unseemly for a man to die fighting in defense of his country."—Homer, *The Iliad*

🎭 "Our obligations to our country never cease but with our lives."—John Adams (1735–1826), letter to Benjamin Rush, April 18, 1808

🎭 "And so, my fellow Americans: ask not what your country can do for you—ask what you can do for your country. My fellow citizens of the world: ask not what America will do for you, but what together we can do for the freedom of man."—John F. Kennedy (1917–1963), Inaugural address, January 20, 1961

🎭 "You're not to be so blind with patriotism that you can't face reality. Wrong is wrong, no matter who does it or says it."—Malcolm X (1925–1965)

🎭 "I only regret that I have but one life to lose for my country."—Nathan Hale (1755–1776), last words, September 22, 1776

Objective: To discern Shakespeare's use of auditory imagery to reinforce his dramatic style in Act IV, scene iii.

🎭 After acting out the remainder of the scene, have the students list the verbs used by Ross that convey auditory imagery.

🎭 Observe how Ross, at first, indirectly tells Macduff the bad news.

🎭 Also, note how Malcolm, one without children, tells Macduff how he should handle his grief in Act IV, scene iii, lines 259, 268–269. Consider Macduff's response: "He has no children" (IV. iii. 255). Briefly discuss whether Macduff refers to Macbeth or Malcolm.

Act V

Objective: To assess how Shakespeare's style informs the reader or viewer about Lady Macbeth from a social/psychological perspective in Act V, scene i.

🎭 Turn off the classroom lights and use a flashlight to imitate the lit candle carried by Lady Macbeth.

🎭 Observe how this scene is spoken in prose, except for the doctor's last speech. Perhaps Shakespeare's shift away from verse reinforces a shift from the norm, another imbalance in a world affected by their crime.

🎭 Reread Lady Macbeth's first and second soliloquy aloud in Act I, scene v, lines 15–33, 45–61. Also, reread her response to the way Macbeth reacts to his bloody hands in Act II, scene ii, lines 82–88. Analyze the following remark that she makes to her husband: "Your constancy / Hath left you unattended" (II. ii. 87–88). Compare her attitude then to her hand washing in Act V, scene i.

- Symbolism: Lady Macbeth commits the murder ostensibly with her eyes open. Discuss the meaning of the doctor and gentlewoman's observation (V. i. 26–27).
- Was Lady Macbeth aware of the consequences of murdering Duncan? Divide the class and have each group argue for or against Lady Macbeth's comprehension of the consequences of her actions. Review her behavior throughout the play.
- Class discussion: Does Lady Macbeth evoke sympathy? Why or why not?

Objective: To analyze character, plot, imagery, and theme in Act V, scenes ii–iii.

- Have your actors read their lines while marching around the classroom and reinforce the importance of the Scottish forces joining with the English army. Like the founding fathers of the United States, the Scottish nobles are rebels and their actions are treasonous. Each side risks its life to oppose a tyrant. Review the language Menteith uses in Act V, scene ii, lines 3–5. Even the dead would rise to fight for such a noble struggle. Angus observes that Macbeth's troops obey out of fear, not out of support for a just cause (V. ii. 22–23).
- Clothing imagery in Act V, scene ii, lines 17–18, 23–25: Create other metaphors and similes to paraphrase Caithness' and Angus' description. As another approach, have students create sports metaphors related to this scene.
- Macbeth falsely savors the comfort of the witches' predictions while the English and Scottish forces coalesce on the doorstep of Dunsinane Castle. Review the evil spirits' predictions in Act IV, scene i, lines 77–139. Ironically, each spirit foreshadows his demise, and Macbeth misinterprets them.

Objective: To read critically by having students create meaningful questions to augment individual understanding.

- ReQuest Procedure: After completing the scene, have students create five questions about the text. These questions can range from a summary of the plot to a higher level interpretation of theme. Go around the room until every student has asked and answered a question. If a student's response is not satisfactory to the questioner, class discussion settles the dispute. This process highlights what students can answer, building self-esteem and contributing to increased student participation (Schoenbach, Greenleaf, Cziko, & Hurwitz, 1999).

Objective: To evaluate leadership qualities or lack thereof among the principal characters Act V, scenes iv–viii. To study the language spoken by the major characters.

- Assess the decisions and remarks the characters make in each of the closing scenes of Act V.

- Consider Malcolm's "hew him down a bough" (V. iv. 6) as a strategy. Is it a sound one?

- Have the students analyze the following lines:

    - Malcolm comments on the rumors abounding that Macbeth is losing support among all sectors of society in Act V, scene iv, lines 14–18.

    - Macduff advises caution in Act V, scene iv, lines 19–21.

    - Siward says that time will tell whether there is a disparity between what they say they have militarily and what they actually can do in Act V, scene iv, lines 22–27.

- Macbeth believes his troops can withstand a siege in Act V, scene v, lines 2–3. Note his personification of "famine and the ague eat[ing] them [his enemies] up" (V. v. 4).

- Evaluate Malcolm's decision to evoke the royal "we" (V. vi. 4) in this brief scene.

- The perception of Macbeth completely turns from an honored hero in Act I to "a title / More hateful" (V. vii. 10–11). Dramatize this act with plastic swords and helmets, if your budget permits. An arrogant Macbeth standing over a fallen Young Siward will maintain classroom focus and understanding in this scene.

- Macduff chooses not to fight the "wretched kerns" (V. vii. 22). Why does he make this decision?

- Does Macbeth develop a conscience when Macduff confronts him in Act V, scene viii, lines 5–7?

- Depending on your time, assign students to memorize and recite dramatically the "Tomorrow" speech (V. v. 22–31), paraphrase the speech, or interpret the metaphors uttered by Macbeth.

- Consider creating sound effects of swords clashing and warriors battling as the students act out the closing scenes.

- Compare Macbeth's words in Act V, scene viii, lines 23–26 to Banquo's advice earlier in the play Act I, scene iii, lines 134–138.

- Malcolm restores order in his closing speech, rewarding the thanes for their loyalty. As an activity, consider having the students modernize the rewards. Ask them to devise a list of rewards they would like to receive. Rewrite Malcolm's speech to reflect the modern era.

- Discuss how Olympic athletes are glorified in our society. Now, determine how war heroes are honored. Compare how society views each award. Does society regard one recipient in a higher stead than the other?

- Small-group activity: Who is more deserving of becoming king: Malcolm or Macduff? (See Handout 13; p. 133.) Create a short drama featuring a group of Scottish thanes discussing who is most worthy of being crowned.

Directing a Production of *Macbeth*: A Brief Overview

A high school production requires a very strong actor in the lead role. Also, I recommend the 10th Edition Arden Shakespeare version of *Macbeth* (Muir, 1992) for its meaningful textual annotations, which are extraordinarily helpful to student actors. Working with a 9-week rehearsal schedule, I divide the play into thirds, concentrating on the first third with blocking, the actual movement of characters across the stage, and memorization before moving onto the middle third. Once the middle third is blocked and memorized, go back and review Sections I and II.

Consider the following as a guideline for a rehearsal schedule:

Section I
- Act I–Act III, scene iii
- Four days blocking
- Four days memory

Section II
- Act III, scene iii–Act IV, scene iii (end at doctor's entrance)
- Four days blocking
- Four days memory
- Memory Review: Act I–Act III, scene iii

Section III
- Act IV, scene iii–Conclusion

- Four days blocking

- Four days memory

- Full Rehearsal

- Four days memory

- Technical and dress rehearsal (which, of course, includes constant memory review)

The practice schedule listed above frontloads the rehearsal so that the last section is not as burdensome on the actors with the performances approaching.

Depending on which scheduling tactic works for you, I recommend that you begin with 4 days of blocking, followed by 4 days of memorization per rehearsal section. Students should have most of a section's play memorized by the third day of memory review. Memory review means that the actors are not using their scripts. They are "off book." Having a student prompter to read missed lines will help move the rehearsal along. This schedule is not unique to *Macbeth*—I have incorporated this structure in each of my 35 productions.

The memory review, comprising Sections I and II (an arbitrary division of the play into thirds) takes 3 days. After completing two thirds of the play, move into the closing third. Once you have finished the memory section, rehearse the play from the beginning again and again. This process respects the time of the actors who have smaller roles and who may leave when their stage time is finished. Also, this process allows for nuanced changes in the closing 2 weeks before the actual production.

Compacting the last section will give the director more time to work on lighting cues and sound cues. Also, there are two sword fights at the end, Macbeth defeating Young Siward and Macduff vanquishing Macbeth. Each fight will need choreographed movements, particularly if real swords (usually fencing swords) are included. The sound of clashing swords captivates the audience. I was fortunate to have a neighbor, an Olympic fencer, train and choreograph the student actors' movements for the fight scenes.

Before auditioning, determine how the stage should look. Of course, the drama department's budget is a reality all high school directors must face. Shakespeare's set may run from the simple to the complex. Of course, having help with set design and construction may be the driving factor in deciding how elaborate the production is. In my plays, student set designers developing and building a set will, of course, increase student participation, which, of course, is the point behind every school production. My students created an elaborate craggy-looking tree, which remained on the stage through every outdoor scene and provided a backdrop for the witches' scenes.

Director's Remarks

Act I

The witches must be mysterious, cackling beings who exude an aura of superstition and magic. Evil and calculating, they are otherworldly. Emphasize the menacing air about them, so that they are malevolent. Overly exaggerated gestures will make them comical. Their costumes should be fluid, moving when they do. Surround them with crashing thunder and crackling lightning. Challenge the tech crew to find solutions for these stage settings. If there is a fog machine available or dry ice, use it to establish a fiendish mood.

Be sure to establish a war hero in the characterization of Macbeth; at the beginning of the play, he squashes a rebellion, fighting bravely and furiously for his king and country. The witches' prophecies should uncover a memory in Macbeth, a deeply buried thought he kept hidden in his brain about being king. This thought now has surfaced and his soliloquies should be delivered with the eagerness of a dieter who has pledged spartan obedience while gorging on ice cream.

Similarly, Lady Macbeth receives the news of Macbeth's encounter with the witches as indisputable fact, never pausing to reflect on its veracity. Her only concern is her husband's mild character, an ironic contrast for an audience who just heard about how Macbeth "unseamed [Macdonwald] from the nave to th' chops" (I. ii. 24). More comparisons abound as King Duncan speaks about the executed Cawdor's betrayal as Macbeth enters. Duncan also observes how pleasant Macbeth's castle is with Banquo concurring.

In Act I, scene vii, Macbeth steps away from the table and delivers a soliloquy expressing his doubts about proceeding with the assassination. Lady Macbeth's combustible intensity needs to surface in this scene. She challenges his manliness and reveals her own ambition. Consider having her slap Macbeth when he haltingly says, "If we should fail" (I. vii. 68).

Act II

The scene opens with Banquo's wandering because of his disturbed sleep. With sleep as a motif, Banquo soon is joined by Macbeth, who tries to garner his political support. Banquo maintains his neutrality. The dagger hallucination should involve Macbeth grasping at air. Revealing a dagger would offer substance to the imaginary. Let the audience see the scene the way it is designed—"a dagger of the mind" (II. i. 50).

In the murder scene in Act II, scene ii, I used a scrim that when lit from the upstage side shows the actors standing behind it. I dimmed the lights and played out the killing of Duncan in shadow, chiaroscuro-style. As soon as Macbeth raises his arm to stab the king, I bathed the scrim from the front in red light. Fade out all the lights and begin the dialogue with Lady Macbeth's remarks. Adding an owl cry or tense music is another way to augment the tension of the drama. Consider voices whispering, "Sleep no more" and "Glamis hath murdered sleep."

As noted in the scene analysis in Chapter 2, the porter scene conveys seriousness in the play that often is overlooked. As the "porter of hell gate" (II. iii. 2) he does stand as a guardian of horror in a microcosm. Of course, he is drunk and unaware of the murder, which just occurred. At the high school level (and other levels as well) playing this scene for laughs is highly appropriate. After the murder scene, perhaps the comic relief is necessary. Also, giving a high school actor an opportunity to "play it big" is usually a crowd pleaser.

The Old Man and Ross should be strolling in Act II, scene iv. Consider breaking the stage-audience wall, beginning with the actors in the audience walking toward the stage. Macduff could enter from the wings and meet them on stage.

Act III

When Macbeth enters he is the king and must behave regally. If possible, have an entourage follow him onstage. Note the "royal we" in the first line of the scene: "Here's our chief guest" (III. i. 11). As the foil to Macbeth, Banquo must appear noble. His "I fear / Thou played'st most foully for 't" (III. i. 2–3) should convey his goodness.

Reinforce the growing divide in the scene between Macbeth and Lady Macbeth. Her harshness should be softened as the audience observes that Macbeth has made decisions without her awareness: "Be innocent of the knowledge, dearest chuck" (III. ii. 51).

Portraying the banquet scene in Act III, scene iv is a challenge that rises or falls with your particular stage arrangement. If you have trap doors, then the task is greatly simplified. If not, then use light and sound to dramatize the ghost of Banquo's movement. Like the dagger, Banquo's ghost is another hallucination. Decide whether you want the audience to see the ghost or not.

Consider the options. Having an actor move across the stage and sit in Macbeth's seat is to dramatize to the audience what Macbeth sees, an approach I advised against in the dagger scene. To portray an empty chair with an agitated and hallucinatory Macbeth is to show the audience what the banquet guests and Lady Macbeth witness, that is, an empty chair.

Because the consensus view among scholars is that Thomas Middleton interpolated the Hecate appearance in Act III, scene v, I do not include it. It is another scene with the witches, which audiences enjoy, but I maintain a more purist tone and choose not to perform it.

Like the Old Man-Ross dialogue in Act II, scene iv, you may choose to break the stage-audience wall with Lennox and the Lord.

Act IV

Hecate's appearance in Act IV does not seem as intrusive as the additional witch scene in Act III, scene v. You should note that some scholars believe that her lines, followed by the "Black Spirits" song are another Middleton contribution.

To convey the evil spirits, I videotaped them ahead of time and dropped a screen in the middle of the action when Macbeth demands to speak to the spirits directly. Practice the timing right and the exchange between Macbeth and the spirits works well. Darken the stage with a spotlight on Macbeth and the effect captures the spookiness of the scene. Add lightning flashes and thunder and the evil ambience is present. When Lennox enters in Act IV, scene i, line 152, remove the screen and raise the lights.

Next is the Macduff castle scene in Act IV, scene ii. The actress who plays Lady Macbeth was disguised as the messenger in my production; obviously, any portrayal is effective here, but I always thought that someone with prior knowledge of the attack would have to be well placed in Macbeth's castle, someone with intimate knowledge of the decision-making process.

Generally, the scene between Macduff and Malcolm has little action. When directing this segment, encourage the characters to move. A few steps stage right or left will suffice. The information exchanged in this scene is pertinent to the plot and helps the audience get a better sense of each character; however, two characters do not need to be sitting during the whole scene. Macduff's reaction needs to be muted. The man is in shock, disbelieving the horrible news that Ross delivers.

Act V

Following the Lady Macbeth sleepwalking opening, the closing act comprises a series of brief action scenes. The actors need to be ready in the wings because there must be a continual flow from scene to scene, leading to the climactic duel between Macbeth and Macduff. In Act V, scene iii, convey a sense of siege with Macbeth and his loyal servant Seyton. Actors with swords and servants should be hurrying back and forth upstage to intensify the action. Malcolm, Siward, and the Scottish nobles need to demonstrate the confidence imbued with those who believe that their cause is just, their strategies purposeful. Conversely, the action inside Macbeth's castle should be panicky and chaotic.

Choreograph the sword fight between Young Siward and Macbeth to make the action dynamic. Dramatize the scene with bold clashing of swords. In addition, the Macbeth-Macduff fight should be intense, too. They, of course, move off stage to complete their battle.

The type of costumes and number of props depend on your budget. Ultimately, the delivery of lines supplemented with lighting and sound will be the factors that will "wow" your audience.

Writing Critically About *Macbeth*

Writing critically about a work of literature in the Advanced Placement, honors, or academic classroom requires a great deal of practice for the student as well as the classroom practitioner. How one teaches writing to students is as individualized as the varied pedagogical practices and strategies that fill the classrooms of neighborhood schools every day. Similar to our teaching practice, we more than likely utilize strategies for writing instruction that were introduced to us in our own secondary and postsecondary schooling. With that being said, we frequently have to monitor and adjust our writing instruction and adapt it to the demands of an ever-changing global society of which our students are living, breathing members.

So, how should you teach writing, specifically writing critically about Shakespeare? There are numerous responses to that query, all of which require the professional expertise and comfort of your own practice. Answering the following questions is a good starting place for doing so:

- What is your attitude about writing?

- How will you be able to teach students of varied writing abilities to create clear and concise prose?

- How can you make these skills transferable throughout each year of their schooling?

Effective writing instruction has equal importance to the English classroom and other content areas, as does any successful analysis of the literature being taught. As our students often bemoan the amount of analytical, argumentative, and expository writing that we ask them to generate, we remind them that if they are going to pursue any level of schooling beyond high school, then effective writing is essential, regardless of one's area of study. Although there are numerous writing texts that encapsulate the writing process for educators, too numerous for our purpose in this chapter, we would direct your attention to William Strunk and E. B. White's seminal work *The Elements of Style* (see Resources section). *The Elements of Style* is a practical and readable text that does not create an overwhelming task for students, but rather provides a clear and cogent resource for easy student access and understanding.

One of the most challenging aspects of teaching English is the amount of student writing that fills our briefcases and school bags. When working with preservice and first-year teachers, we always recommend developing the proper grading attitude about writing assignments. Considering smaller and more frequent assignments certainly gives students more practice and teachers less burdensome stacks of papers to grade. There are a number of in-class writing prompts in Chapter 2 for your use. Another quick stress reliever is to incorporate more peer editing. The advantage of student grading is that students write more frequently while shifting the grading burden away from the teacher. The stack of unread essays eventually will dwindle, but the most important, and oftentimes the most challenging, aspect of writing instruction is the fatigue level of the reader. How many of us have gotten to the last eight papers in a stack of fair to average essays and wished them to be complete? In this chapter, there are some helpful strategies, tips, and activities in effective writing instruction to lessen the stress level that is brought about by hundreds and hundreds of essay pages that *need* to be graded right now!

The first part of this chapter spells out some strategies for teaching analytical/argumentative/expository writing through an examination of rhetorical strategies and their uses in writing. We will delve into a few major rhetorical elements namely exigence, audience, and purpose. The five-paragraph essay model, a cogent and sometimes maligned model for writing, will be used as the organizational pattern. To aid in the organization of the essay, see the diagram in Figure 3. Figures 4 and 5 will guide the peer editing process. The evaluation sheet in Figure 4 allows student editors to cite three things about the essay that they like/agree with (+), three things about the essay that may be unclear/need revision (-), and three questions the editor would pose to the author (?).

The Basics of Writing Instruction: Interplay of Rhetoric

When discussing writing with secondary and postsecondary students, some famous words from the English philosopher and Enlightenment thinker John Locke are apropos. He wrote, "Rhetoric is that powerful instrument of error and

FIVE-PARAGRAPH ESSAY PLAN

THESIS STATEMENT:

TOPIC SENTENCE:

TOPIC SENTENCE:

TOPIC SENTENCE:

TOPIC SENTENCE:

Figure 3. Five paragraph essay plan.

Advanced Placement Classroom: Macbeth © Prufrock Press • This page may be photocopied or reproduced with permission for classroom use.

Peer Editing Evaluation Sheet

NAME OF AUTHOR _____

NAME OF EDITOR _____

+

1.)

2.)

3.)

_____

—

1.)

2.)

3.)

_____

?

1.)

2.)

3.)

_____

Figure 4. Peer editing evaluation sheet.

The Peer Editing Top 10

1. Is the paper in MLA format? Be sure to check for a title, an appropriate heading, and correct citation format.

2. How effective is the thesis statement/paragraph? Is the author arguing a "why" question? Is the argument precise/concise?

3. Is there paragraph coherence? Does each paragraph have effective transitions?

4. How does the author utilize his or her conclusion? Is the conclusion a summation of the analysis that was presented, or rather a restatement of the thesis without delineating a "so what" conclusion?

5. Is there an overabundance of plot summary?

6. Does the author utilize literary present tense when discussing the action in the story/play/essay? For example, "Hamlet *is*" not "Hamlet *was.*"

7. Does the author use active voice?

    "The boy hit the ball" →   Active
    "The ball was hit by the boy" →   Passive

8. Does the author assume information about the audience and apply "I" or "we" to his or her argument? If so, it should be informal third person, such as "The reader . . ."

9. Does the author digress from his or her argument?

10. Has the author proofread his or her work? (Spell check is not the same as proofreading!)

Figure 5. Peer editing top 10 list.

deceit." Although Locke had a low opinion of rhetoric as a tool of trickery and dishonesty, rhetoric certainly drives our world's economy, influences voters, and more pragmatically (should) fill the pages of student writing. Sadly, our students have virtually lost this art in their speaking and writing and see rhetoric as a tool that politicians manipulate each time they run for public office or advertisers employ as a way to sell us an item that we never knew we needed until now. Yet, our politicians, some of the most adroit manipulators of rhetorical strategies, are not the figures that our students relate to; rather, it is the influence of the media on rhetoric with whom our students can most often connect. Today's adolescents are surrounded by rhetoric in every facet of their lives. When they turn on a television, log-on to the Internet, or open up a magazine, they are bombarded with manipulative language. Discussing modern media provides immediacy to the topic of rhetoric in our students' lives. To further this point, the first writing assignment with my students is to find and evaluate an advertisement in a magazine, focusing on the rhetorical strategies and their effectiveness.

Today's children are even more susceptible to media influence, not having reached an appropriate age when the discernment skills to differentiate between fact and fiction have fully developed. Have you ever watched a network that plays children's cartoons and commercials? I have often taped a few of these commercials to demonstrate the manipulation of rhetorical strategies on our youngest consumers. My sons are both under the age of 5 and influenced by myriad commercials. They are labeled consumers even though each has no career path and/ or job. As consumers, they watch these commercials and are wowed by the superheroes and action figures that fly across the screen. When their birthdays approach and their grandparents, aunts, and uncles purchase birthday presents, most likely something that they have witnessed come to life on a commercial, the reality of the product is very different from the promise of the commercial. What message is this sending our very youngest consumers? Students can easily relate to rhetoric when it is put in this context.

Rhetoric tends to manipulate the audience of television commercials; however, when used effectively, it can produce a speech or essay that can be inspirational for individuals and maybe even revolutionize global thinking. Henry David Thoreau's "Resistance to Civil Government" is one such rhetorical essay, which has been an inspiration to millions of individuals. In 1849, because Thoreau was against slavery and the Mexican War, he did not pay his poll tax. Great minds such as Mahatma Gandhi, Martin Luther King, Jr., and Nelson Mandela changed their own worlds based on Thoreau's rhetorical reasoning. The great Roman orator and rhetorician Marcus Tullius Cicero discerned language used by the skilled orator as an individual talent and not, as Locke's opinion would lead us to believe, as a fraudulent deception. Cicero said, "Nothing is so unbelievable that oratory cannot make it acceptable." Rhetoric is the art of using language effectively and persuasively, and to those ends, our students' writing also should reflect these ideas.

Three Crucial Rhetorical Elements:
Exigence, Audience, and Purpose

A number of years ago, I attended an Advanced Placement conference at DePaul University in Chicago, lead by Dr. David A. Jolliffe, currently the Brown Chair in English Literacy and an English professor at the University of Arkansas. Jolliffe has written numerous books on writing and rhetoric and provided some practical advice to the educators attending the conference about approaches to the teaching of writing. One of the many cogent ideas that I took from that conference that always has influenced my instruction of writing is the word *exigence*. Exigence is the need or a gap that requires a textual response or calls an individual to say or do something. For example, if my school district decided that all of our students would have to wear uniforms at the beginning of this school year, there would be an outcry of frustration and possible anger. The immediate response on behalf of the parents and students is the kernel of exigence, but when that reaction leads to a textual response, this activity reflects the true nature of exigence. When individuals complain about something, but do not act upon it, it does not fulfill our definition. Therefore, when one of our incoming 12th graders, who felt as though her classmates' freedom of expression and individuality were being suppressed, wrote a letter to the local paper and the school newspaper decrying the "evils" of the new uniform policy, she demonstrated exigence. In laymen's terms, Jolliffe explained, "Exigence is the reaction people have when something gets stuck in their craw." The idea that something spurs us to write is the basis for all good writing. When Patrick Henry stated, "I know not what course others may take; but as for me, give me liberty or give me death!" to the Virginia Provincial Convention in 1775 after years of salutary neglect and extreme taxation by Great Britain, I am sure that he was not doubting how he felt about being ruled by the British. In the same vein, Franklin Delano Roosevelt was certain of his foreign policy stance during his speech on December 8, 1941, while asking for the Congress to declare war on Japan the day after the bombing of Pearl Harbor. In each of these proclamations, and there are thousands of other examples similar to these famous speeches, the orator had a high level of exigence. Something, or someone, committed an act and because of this, something needed to be done, and for our purposes, a written response is required.

Exigence is a fundamental idea for students to understand about their own writing process as they search for their own critical voice. Students frequently wonder, "How is impending death/danger of war the same as my three-page paper on Lady Macbeth? Who cares what I have to say?" Quite frankly, we remind them that if they do not care about what they are writing or have no exigence for their subject, then why should the reader care what they have to say? One of the cardinal errors in poor student writing is that the exigence is either completely missing, or worst of all, the students feel disconnected from the subject matter. Devoid of the student's critical voice, the essay is either a plot summation or a regurgitation of what the instructor may have already said in the classroom.

The topic of exigence leads us to our next points about understanding the audience and the purpose for writing. In academic writing, students believe that they are writing for the classroom teacher, and that the purpose of their writing assignment is to receive an A. Yet, this outcome is not always the case. What if the teacher wanted to share the work with the author's classmates, their peers in other classes, or even the author's parents? Can it be possible that the student essay could in fact change the world or, at the very least, the way individuals think about a subject matter?

Too often students become familiar with what a teacher "looks for" while he or she grades a paper and the students write for that particular audience while feeling as though their words lack any purpose other than to complete the assignment. The problem with this technique, although it may be successful during a school year for a specific teacher, is that the students will then be forced to write for a changing audience each time they write. Although many of us have had teachers and professors in our schooling who have spent time on a specific criterion of the writing process, we should not follow this technique as successful pedagogy. We should push students to ask themselves in their drafting process, "To whom are you speaking?" and "Why am I writing this?" If that response is a peer on the other end of a text message or e-mail, then the audience and purpose of the writing product will greatly differ from an analytical response to *Macbeth*. In the drafting process of an essay, students should never wonder to whom they are writing, and why they choose to do so. A key purpose as English teachers is to focus students to think critically about literature and to reflect and respond to the works in our varied curricula.

Demystifying the Thesis:
Making Arguments Clearer

One of the most confusing elements of writing for students at the secondary and postsecondary levels is how to generate a thesis paragraph. Although there are some very creative and effective pedagogical approaches to writing, one major point of confusion for students is the thesis/introductory paragraph. Generating an effective thesis paragraph is the most important and essential factor in the formation of an argument. Yet, at the core and foundation of any successful argument is a solid, clear, and focused reason; in other words—the thesis statement. Scholars and writing instructors tend to debate where the thesis statement should be placed in a student's essay. For novice writers and students struggling with structural and organizational patterns in writing, the thesis statement should always be the last sentence of their thesis paragraph. However, students may choose to produce "the delayed thesis statement" approach wherein the writer may wait until the concluding paragraph to present his or her central idea, choosing to focus on the logical progression of the argument in the essay's body. My disagreement with presenting this option to the neophyte writer is that he or she may have a very weak or unclear understanding of the interplay of rhetoric, reasoning, and logic as the thesis is formulated for analytical, argumentative, and expository writing.

The Why of Argumentation and the Courtroom Motif

The central rhetorical question that the thesis statement clearly needs to address is "Why?" At the heart of argumentation is a response to why things do or do not occur. These are the higher level thinking skills of analyzing, evaluating, and creating labeled in Bloom's taxonomy. The term *critical thinking* often is extolled in secondary and postsecondary classrooms, and an examination of the writing process will lend further credence to an educator's effective pedagogy in critical thinking proficiency for students.

Students often are uncertain about the practical application of critical and analytical thinking in their everyday lives. The first example that I share with my students to aid them in visualizing the "Why?" question in argumentation is a courtroom setting. Many students have seen television and movie courtroom dramas and are aware of the courtroom structure and how well or poorly lawyers present their case to the jury by means of varied rhetorical strategies. Writing an analytical, argumentative, and expository essay is no different than a lawyer in the courtroom presenting his or her opening argument. This function defines the thesis paragraph. If a lawyer's opening words to the jury are, "Here is Joey, he did not do it. More to come," I am sure that our fictional Joey will be in serious trouble if that is his defense. Rather, we want students to see the value in argumentation and the ability of the individual who is setting forth his or her argument. Why is Joey innocent? Why did he not commit the crime? How did he act in similar circumstances?

The thesis paragraph is similar to the lawyer's opening statement, allowing the jurors to hear about Joey's innocence while at the same time presenting the argumentative structure for the lawyer's case. Oftentimes courtroom trials, especially murder cases, are filled with evidence and experts testifying on both sides of the bar; however, students need to be able to stand on their own two argumentative feet and clearly present their rationale for why they believe what they do.

The courtroom is a great classroom model for argumentation coming to life. The supporting paragraphs are the foundation and evidence provided by the lawyer, while the closing argumentation should be the summation of all the major ideas. We have included a classroom activity that re-creates a courtroom setting in a discussion of *Macbeth* in Chapter 8 (see Activity 19: "Macbeth on Trial: Creative Debate"; p. 148).

Peer Editing and Peer Review Groups

We would be remiss if we did not spend some time reviewing the importance of the drafting process, peer editing, and essay revision in peer review groups. One of the biggest challenges for students in expressing themselves is to give and receive criticism about their writing, especially from peers. Students often will balk at having to share their writing with the "non-teacher" and when directed to do so, can be remiss about how to provide constructive criticism to their peers. There is a direct correlation in the classroom between working with peer editors and aiding students to write confidently and discover their voice. The self-assurance and confidence only can flourish in a situation where student writers and peer editors understand their task for editing, and the writing environment can be one of trial and error. The writing partnership that evolves among classroom writers and peer reviewers needs to follow clearly stipulated focus points. The following are a few focus points that peer editors should consider when reviewing an essay:

- Does the essay have a clear and focused thesis answering "Why?" or "How so?"

- Are there logical body paragraphs that connect with effective transitional phrases?

- Are there good topic sentences in the supporting paragraphs that serve as mini-thesis statements?

- Does the essay contain effective vocabulary that pertains to the subject?

- Is the writing clear and concise, developing and moving the argument along rather than filling pages with, as Hamlet would say, "Words, words, words"?

- Is there a solid conclusion that answers a "So what?" question? (So what have we learned? So what do we do now? So now that my mind has been steered in this way, how does it impact future reaction papers about the text?)

Writing About *Macbeth*: A Practical Example

Reconsidering Malcolm: Is Order Truly Restored to Scotland?

As argued in Chapter 4, King Duncan's naming of his eldest son Malcolm as Prince of Cumberland not only goes against the rules of the tanistry established by the Scottish clans, but it also changes the very existence of these clannish leaders from the traditional Scottish title thane to the English title of earl. The Renaissance audience needed to experience closure and a restoration of order in each play; therefore, Shakespeare considered it a necessity to provide resolution to his plays and ultimately, in the case of *Macbeth*, install Malcolm as the rightful heir to the throne, as established by Duncan, the deceased and usurped monarch of Scotland.

In order to develop higher level thinking skills in all classrooms, students need to be able to examine both sides of the following arguments. For example:

- Is Scotland better with the leadership of Malcolm?

- Would the thanes be happy that their generations of Scottish identity change from the clannish thane to the English earl?

- Maybe Malcolm is the likely successor to the butchery of Macbeth, but then again what experience does he have?

- Would Scotland and her warrior culture be better served with the warrior Macduff, the man who slays the monstrous Macbeth, rather than an untested and youthful prince? (For an in-depth, higher level thinking activity that explores these questions, see Chapter 8, Assignment 18: Will the Real Tanist Please Stand Up?; p. 147)

These are a few of the many questions that can and should arise in the *Macbeth* classroom at the play's conclusion. When generating analytical, argumentative, and expository essays about the play, the classroom practitioner must serve as a guide for educational risk taking. As teachers many of our best lessons are equal parts great pedagogical training accompanied by educational risk taking. We need not forget that our students and their connection to their writing is an analogous situation. Allowing the classroom to serve as a trampoline when students fall, rather than a concrete floor, will guide them away from rote responses. Consequently, guided practice, brainstorming, prewriting, drafting, peer review/revision, and final publication will produce clear and coherent writing that far exceeds formulaic composition theories and stock ideas about how to teach writing. Be as open to the writing process and the varied responses of your students throughout the writing process, as you hope that they will be during your teaching of *Macbeth*.

Student Activities and Differentiated Instruction

The following activities, designed to differentiate instruction in your classroom, appeal to a variety of learning styles and multiple intelligences. These research-based, metacognitive activities have been successfully implemented in our secondary and postsecondary classrooms. In utilizing the suggestions in this chapter and throughout *Advanced Placement Classroom: Macbeth*, the educator needs to know the diverse learning styles and ability levels of his or her students. Even in an Advanced Placement classroom setting, students are individuals, not interchangeable cogs. The challenge for all educators is to modify the curriculum to the student, not force the student to fit the curriculum.

Although there are curricular and budgetary restraints, the fundamental reason educators need to differentiate is to ensure that learning is taking place and that instruction is responsive and reflective (Tomlinson, 2003). C. A. Tomlinson wrote:

> To teach most effectively, teachers must take into account *who* they are teaching as well as *what* they are teaching. The goal of the differentiated classroom is to plan actively and consistently to help each learner move as far and as fast as possible along a learning continuum. (pp. 1–2)

Activity 1: Why Shakespeare?
Prior Knowledge Assessment of Shakespeare

Why Shakespeare? One of the first activities in this text is to gauge the responses of your students to this very question. Be open to the prior knowledge activity; you may be surprised by the students' varied responses. Allow students the freedom to bash the Bard a little bit. Shakespeare's audiences were so diverse that he knew that citizens of varying tastes and educational backgrounds attended his productions.

The William Shakespeare K-W-L Chart and the Shakespearean Who's Who nametags (Handouts 1 and 2) tap into the students' knowledge bank from any previous study of the Bard. The K-W-L chart, a brainstorming graphic organizer, asks students what they already know (K) about a topic, what they want (W) to know, and what they have already learned (L) at the end of a unit. The first two columns of this chart provide structure to future lessons. However, to allow for formative assessment each day in your classroom, it may be a good idea to remind the students to keep their charts with their daily class materials. Only partially based on an evaluation of their prior knowledge, the effectiveness of the K-W-L chart is centered on their willingness to learn about a topic. The last bracket, which will not be filled in during this lesson, provides the direction of your unit for the student. At the midpoint or end of your unit of study, ask the students to complete the final column. Did they learn what they had anticipated? Were all of the anticipated ideas and themes discussed? If not, why not?

What You Will Need

- A bucket/coffee tin
- A number of yellow sticky note pads
- Copies of William Shakespeare K-W-L Chart (see Handout 1).
- Copies of the Shakespearean Who's Who? (see Handout 2).

Activity Explained

1. Prior to the students entering the classroom, copy the William Shakespeare K-W-L Chart, as well as the sheet with the character nametags on it. (We have placed 20 nametags on the sheet. You may have more students in your classroom: If so, be sure that there are not more than three students in the different groups). Cut the nametags, fold them, and place them in your bucket/coffee tin.

2. As the students enter your classroom, have them choose one of the character nametags from the container. Ask them not to reveal their new identity until all students have a nametag. This character nametag will place students in groups based on characters of Shakespearean plays that they may have read or viewed prior to coming to your class. The plays that

we have selected are: *Romeo and Juliet*, *Julius Caesar*, *The Merchant of Venice*, and *A Midsummer Night's Dream*. If your students have not read these plays, you will want to include Shakespearean titles that are in your school's curriculum to replace the unfamiliar plays.

3. When the students are in their groups, check to see if they are able to identify and discuss the play associated with their character's name. Distribute a number of sticky notes to the various groups. On the sticky note they will be asked to write down a piece of information about Shakespeare. The writing may include words, ideas about a specific play, his life, his writing—anything about Shakespeare. At this point in the brainstorming process, distribute the K-W-L Chart to your students. The students should complete the first column while they are filling out their sticky notes and then complete the second column independently to acknowledge what they want to learn.

4. When each group has filled out at least 7–10 sticky notes, as well as its K-W-L chart, ask a representative from each group to come to the front of the classroom and stick these brainstormed ideas on the blackboard/white board. After placing them on the board, ask the students to return to their seats.

5. After each group had placed its brainstorming notes on the board, ask a few students to help you organize the ideas into categories, taking down all repeats. Remember that no point is irrelevant or wrong. Allow the students to take risks before the unit begins.

6. Read the student responses aloud and discuss them. This activity, which is informal and fun, will serve as your springboard for the larger questions of this lesson.

7. After you have discussed the brainstorming activity, shift the discussion to the higher level idea of "Why Shakespeare?" We always recommend that before embarking on a higher level discussion with students that you allow the students about 5–7 minutes to formulate their response in writing. To keep them on-task, be sure to remind them that they will be asked to read their writing to their peers.

Name: _____

Date: _____

Handout 1: William Shakespeare K-W-L Chart

WHAT I ALREADY *KNOW*	WHAT I *WANT* TO KNOW	WHAT I HAVE *LEARNED*

Advanced Placement Classroom: Macbeth © Prufrock Press • This page may be photocopied or reproduced with permission for classroom use.

Handout 2: Shakespearean Who's Who?

Romeo	Romeo
Juliet	Juliet
Mercutio	Mercutio
The Nurse	The Nurse
Friar Lawrence	Friar Lawrence
Julius Caesar	Julius Caesar
Brutus	Brutus
Antonio	Antonio
Shylock	Shylock
Portia	Portia
Oberon	Oberon
Bottom	Bottom

Activity 2: *Macbeth* Unit Learning Goals Contract

At the beginning of a teaching unit, consider including a goals-oriented contract in your classroom. Marzano, Pickering, and Pollock (2001) examined the value of the teacher involving the student in setting the learning goals at the beginning of a unit, monitoring and adjusting these goals in concert with the introduction of new knowledge, and evaluating how well these goals were met. The *Macbeth* Unit Learning Goals Contract in Handout 3 offers defined objectives for each student in the classroom. Specific requirements allow students to set goals for their learning that the teacher may easily verify.

Activity Explained

1. This is an optional activity. If you choose to have your students complete a contract, you may give them the contract we have provided in Handout 3 or create your own specific to your goals.
2. Students should be given the contract prior to beginning the study of the play. It usually is best to have them read over the goals and sign the contract in class to ensure you receive a contract from each student.

Name: _____ Date: _____

Handout 3:
Macbeth Unit Learning Goals Contract

As a student in this class, I, _____, will do my best to reach the following learning goals upon the completion of my study of Macbeth.

Below is a list of goals that my teacher has set out to achieve in this unit:

At the completion of this unit on *Macbeth*, the student will be able to:
- Identify personal learning goals
- Demonstrate prior knowledge about Shakespearean drama
- Self-assess progress toward the respective learning goals of the unit
- Understand and analyze the nuances in *Macbeth*
- Listen to an audio version of various speeches in *Macbeth*
- Define ambition and soliloquy
- Critique various characters in the play, focusing on Macbeth's tragic downfall
- Demonstrate an understanding of the play through various differentiated learning activities
- Debate Macbeth's responsibility for the play's tragic outcome
- Perform various scenes from *Macbeth*
- Evaluate how well learning goals were achieved
- Successfully complete a unit assessment on *Macbeth*

I have met these learning goals through the following activities:

✓
✓
✓
✓

At the end of the Macbeth *unit, I feel as though I have met the following goals:*

✓
✓
✓
✓

At the completion of this unit on Macbeth, *I now can apply my new learning in the following ways:*

✓
✓
✓
✓

Activities 3 and 4: Shakespearean Structured Note-Taking and Soliloquy Semantic Map

A key skill in a technologically based society is the ability to manage information in an efficient and organized manner. Inundated with information in secondary and postsecondary classrooms, students are expected to perceive and process details well. A great deal of educational research has been devoted to the efficacy of student note-taking correlating with success in the classroom. Researchers have advocated for the importance of a structured note-taking system as a significant teaching methodology (Beecher & ERIC Clearinghouse, 1988). Billmeyer and Barton (2002) reinforced these ideas:

> Using a note-taking system that assists in recall and retention of information is essential. Structured note-taking is one of a variety of note-taking strategies; however, it offers students a visual framework that can help them determine just which information to include as they take notes. [...] Eventually, as students practice this skill, they learn to devise their own graphic organizer. (p. 137)

The two note-taking strategies in Handouts 4 and 5 are examples of structured note-taking and semantic mapping in a study of *Macbeth*. These techniques will guide student thinking and classroom discussions in a higher level framework. Handout 6 is a semantic map template that you may modify for your own classroom purposes.

Activity Explained

1. Take students through the examples provided for note-taking, explaining how organizing their notes can help them study better.
2. Provide blank copies to the students for their use as they read the play.
3. You may choose to check notes periodically by having students organize their notes in folders or binders.

Handout 4: Comedy vs. Tragedy Note-Taking Example

Comedy vs. Tragedy

WHAT IS A TRAGEDY?

- Protagonist is likable to the audience, yet has a "tragic flaw"

- "Tragic flaw" more than likely leads to the protagonist's downfall; always the potential for good and evil

- Most, if not all, of the major characters are dead at the end of the play, through treachery, deceit, dishonesty, suicide, etc.

- Restoration of order

FAMOUS COMEDIES

- *Much Ado About Nothing*
- *A Midsummer Night's Dream*

FAMOUS TRAGEDIES

- *King Lear*
- *Romeo and Juliet*

WHAT IS A COMEDY?

- Young lovers overcome a conflict by the play's conclusion, brought about by elder members of society

- Mistaken identity

- Normally ends in marriage for unmarried characters

- Restoration of order

Handout 5: Soliloquy Semantic Map Example

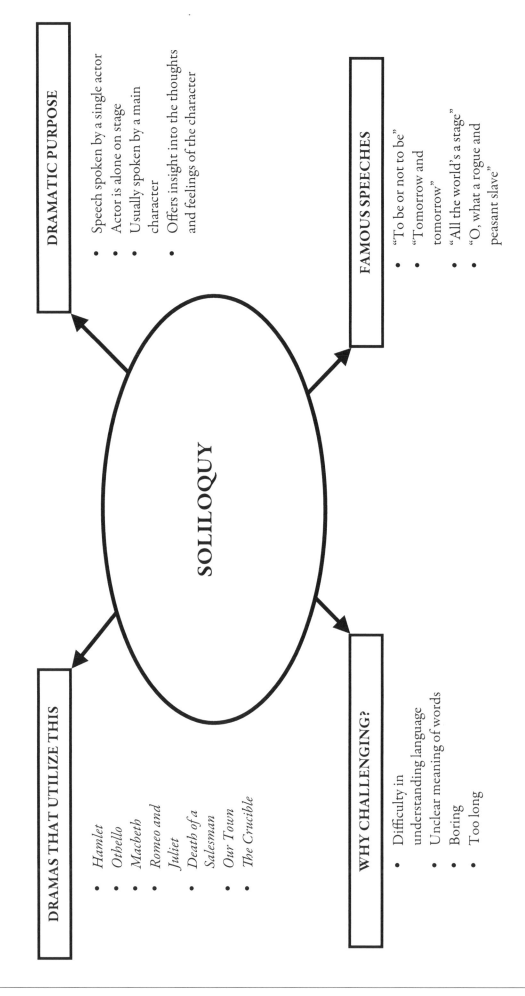

DRAMATIC PURPOSE

- Speech spoken by a single actor
- Actor is alone on stage
- Usually spoken by a main character
- Offers insight into the thoughts and feelings of the character

FAMOUS SPEECHES

- "To be or not to be"
- "Tomorrow and tomorrow"
- "All the world's a stage"
- "O, what a rogue and peasant slave"

SOLILOQUY

DRAMAS THAT UTILIZE THIS

- *Hamlet*
- *Othello*
- *Macbeth*
- *Romeo and Juliet*
- *Death of a Salesman*
- *Our Town*
- *The Crucible*

WHY CHALLENGING?

- Difficulty in understanding language
- Unclear meaning of words
- Boring
- Too long

Handout 6: Blank Semantic Map Example

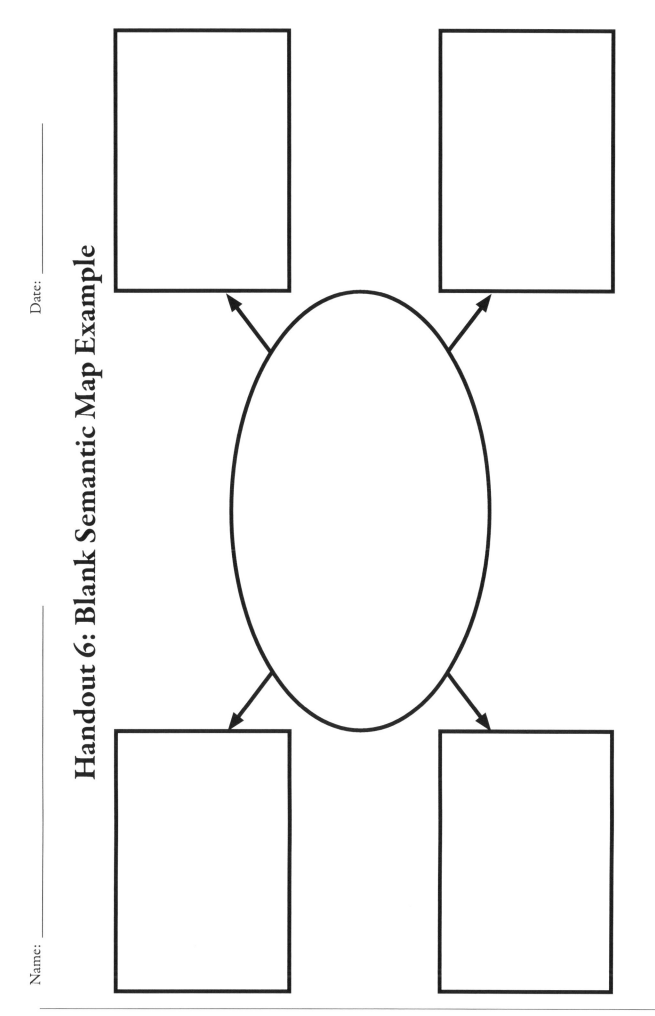

Activity 5: The "Historical" Macbeth Informational Search

Students need to understand the history behind the plot of *Macbeth*. You may want to share some of the information we have already provided in this book. Alternatively, this activity allows the students to uncover the historical information on their own.

Activity Explained

1. Give students the following prompt:

   Today, you are a Scottish historian uncovering the truth and rumors about King Macbeth. The University of Inverness has charged you with the task of discovering the "true Macbeth": separating the reality from the dramatic tale woven by William Shakespeare.

   Your research should be typed, in MLA format, and include a works cited of all source material that you have uncovered. Your historical findings will need to be supported by:
   - five well-researched Web sites,
   - four textual or database resources, and
   - three quotations from Shakespeare's *Macbeth*.

2. After explaining the prompt, give students Handout 7, which provides the criteria for their search. They will need access to the library or the Internet. You may choose to have them complete this activity in groups if you have few computer stations.

3. Instruct students to answer each question on a separate piece of paper (or in a typed document), attaching the required images and map behind their answers.

Handout 7:
The "Historical" Macbeth Informational Search

(10) _____ Contrast the literary Macbeth to his historical counterpart. Indicate three specific differences.

(5) _____ Attach a map that identifies Macbeth's region of origin, as well as sections of his kingdom that he ruled. Be sure that each area of the map is colorful, clear, and accurate. (You may draw your own map.)

(10) _____ Attach two images that relate to any aspect of Macbeth's 11th-century life.

(5) _____ Mention three historically accurate events that reflect King Macbeth's positive leadership.

(10) _____ What were some of the challenges that Macbeth faced in his life?

(10) _____ Completed works cited page in MLA format.

(50) _____

Activities 6 and 7: Ambition Synectic and Synectic Summary: *Macbeth*

Synectic summaries are graphic organizers with the purpose of defining words or summarizing ideas using very dissimilar or apparently opposite words: "By using synectics, people's divergent thinking and capacity for solving problems increase" (Hummell, 2006, p. 22). Rick Wormeli (2005) views the use of synectics with students in the following way:

> The premise for using synectics as a summarizing technique is to have students look at the critical attributes of something under study in unusual ways and, through this unconventional analysis, come away with a deeper understanding of it than they would have gotten from a quick "define the terms" type of assignment. (p. 160)

In the classroom setting educators are very focused on defining keywords or ideas. Even in the English classroom, which deals much more with the subjective than the objective, empirical knowledge is still an important part of our pedagogy.

Although we have provided synectics that seek to define the word *ambition* and compare Macbeth to an animal, it is our hope, as with many of the other blank graphic organizers that we have attached, that you will create your own synectics while working with your students.

Activity Explained

1. Distribute the Ambition Synectic (Handout 8) or the Synectic Summary: Macbeth (Handout 10) to students and assign them to a partner. (Handout 9 is a blank chart for your use.) For this activity to work well, students should not be in groups of more than two. Ask the pairs to spend approximately 15 minutes to complete the synectic summaries.

2. After an appropriate amount of time has elapsed, depending on the size and academic prowess of the group, have them share their ideas among the large group. You may want to have a blank synectic on the chalkboard, whiteboard, or overhead and fill in the student ideas as the discussion develops. Stress the importance of completing the diagram. As they fill in the organizers, remind them that they are synthesizing new definitions from the original dictionary definition and creating new comparisons for the character of Macbeth.

Name: _____

Date: _____

Handout 8: Ambition Synectic

Definition	*Similar To* What words have the same or similar meaning?	*Feels Like* What would it feel like to have the characteristics or traits of . . .?	*Opposite To* What words have the opposite meaning or characteristics?	*Similar To* What words have the same or similar meaning?	*Synthesis* Now, put it all together to create new definitions.

Name: _____

Date: _____

Handout 9: Blank Synectic

_____ Synectic

Definition	Similar To	Feels Like	Opposite To	Similar To	Synthesis
	Similar To What words have the same or similar meaning?	*Feels Like* What would it feel like to have the characteristics or traits of . . .?	*Opposite To* What words have the opposite meaning or characteristics?	*Similar To* What words have the same or similar meaning?	*Synthesis* Now, put it all together to create new definitions.

Advanced Placement Classroom: Macbeth © Prufrock Press • This page may be photocopied or reproduced with permission for classroom use.

Name: _____   Date: _____

Handout 10:
Synectic Summary: Macbeth

How Is Macbeth Like Each of These Animals?

Elephant	Lion
Chameleon	**Snake**

Activity 8: *Macbeth* Role Play

The *Macbeth* Role Play activity provides students with an opportunity to select and "become" a character from the play. Hearkening back to Ancient Greek theater or the Elizabethan masquerade, this activity has a more modern connection, namely the weekly segment from the popular and humorous ESPN rapid-fire sports talk show called "Pardon the Interruption" (PTI). The hosts of the show, holding enlarged photos of sports and media celebrities on sticks, respond to questions that relate to the celebrity's lifestyle or profession. During this segment viewers often will hear "responses" from cutout images of famous people. Like any new activity, students will become engaged with practice.

What You Will Need

- Art supplies, particularly pipe cleaners and colored yarn
- Paper and scissors
- Large paint stirring sticks
- Heavy duty tape

Activity Explained

1. Working in pairs, students will select characters' names from a box. Make sure that there is a representative list of characters for them to choose.
2. Each pair will design characters and prepare for an interview.
3. Questions will come from the students working together as a class before the creation of characters begins, or you may wish to play host and develop a list of questions yourself.

Activities 9 and 10: Soliloquy Think-Aloud and Open Up the Keeley Doors

The pedagogical strategy called "think-alouds" demonstrates to the student how the teacher "thinks through" a text as he or she is reading. This teacher-as-model approach is a very valuable teaching methodology because "[the] students see how the teacher attempts to construct meaning for unfamiliar vocabulary, engages in dialogue with the author, or recognizes when she isn't comprehending and selects a fix-up strategy that addresses a problem that she is having" (Billmeyer & Barton, 2002, p. 139). Our version of the think-aloud strategy can be found in Handout 11. This handout can be used with the activity that follows.

Based on Lori Oczkus' (Oczkus & International Reading Association, 2003) The Fabulous Four activity, Open Up the Keeley Doors is a process that encourages critical reading through active involvement with a sample text, asking students to predict, question, clarify, and summarize a passage. Handout 12 contains the Open Up the Keeley Doors template and can be used with the activity that follows.

Activity Explained

1. Depending on your time, this activity may last from 15–40 minutes. You may select to use either Handout 11 or Handout 12 with this activity.

2. Have students read through Macbeth's "Tomorrow" soliloquy (V. v. 22–31) in 15 seconds. Students briefly write some predictions based on the quick read. Students then should turn to a classmate and discuss their predictions.

3. Next, students should reread the text again for 45 seconds. Students may underline or highlight key words. What words or phrases stand out? Which images are difficult to comprehend? Which ones are easy to understand? Again, either have students share with a classmate or get responses from the whole class.

4. Students look at the text again for a minute, notating reactions in the margins or highlighting key points. This section consists of "I wonder" or "I think" remarks, questioning the meaning of Macbeth's speech in the play's context. Discuss as a class.

5. Have the class reread the text again for 2 minutes, focusing on key ideas. Tell them to write key words or phrases that represent what Macbeth means in his famous soliloquy. Students should turn to a partner and discuss the passage's meaning, then share their analysis with the rest of the class.

Handout 11: "Tomorrow" Soliloquy Think-Aloud

Making Connections	Visualizing	Predicting	Summarizing	Identifying Main Idea
What feelings, personal experiences, and other texts can we relate to while reading this passage from *Macbeth*?	What scene does Macbeth create? How do we visualize the setting?	What is the next event(s) to follow? What might Macbeth be like? What might Lady Macbeth be like?	What is Macbeth saying in this passage about himself? About humanity?	What is the theme or intention of Shakespeare in this passage? What does he inform us about Macbeth?

Name: _____ Date: _____

Handout 12:
Open Up the Keeley Doors

Directions: Copy Macbeth's "Tomorrow" speech and paste it in the center of a tri-folded piece of printer paper. Fold the left and right side in so that each side covers the "Tomorrow" speech. On the outside left fold, write, "Predict" and below that write "Clarify." On the right fold write "Question" and below that, write "Summarize." An example is below.

PREDICT:		**QUESTION:**
(Fold)----------	****Print the text of the "Tomorrow" soliloquy here.***	*(Fold)*-----------
CLARIFY:		**SUMMARIZE:**

Activity 11: Malcolm and Macduff Venn Diagram

The Venn diagram, a widely used graphic organizer for comparing and contrasting characters, concepts, and themes, is a very effective teaching tool because it encourages students to see visual representations of their responses. The purpose of this Venn diagram is to aid in the prewriting process, providing a springboard for the organization of ideas. Students should use Handout 13 to compare and contrast the characters of Malcolm and Macduff. Handout 14 provides a blank Venn diagram for you to assign other character or scene comparisons.

Activity Explained

1. Provide each student with a copy of Handout 13.
2. Have the students work through the scenes that contain Malcolm and Macduff and write down attributes of their individual characters and those they share. You may wish to have them do this in the context of determining who would be the best future king for Scotland.

Name: _____

Date: _____

Handout 13:
Comparing and Contrasting Malcolm and Macduff Venn Diagram

Handout 14:
Blank Venn Diagram

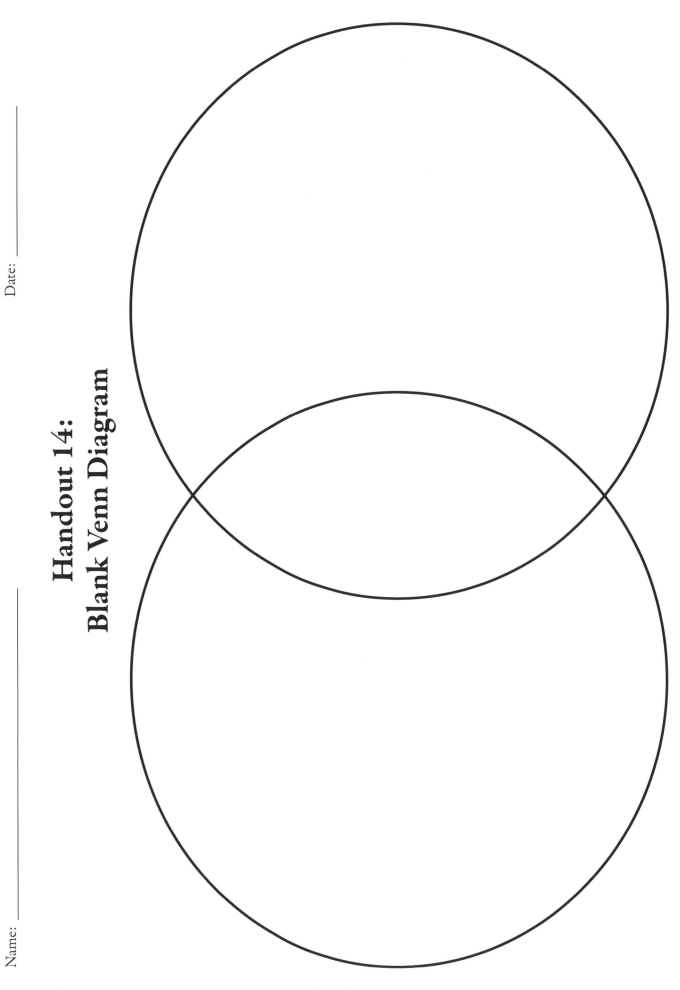

Activity 12: Character Body
Analogy Connection Chart

The Character Body Analogy Connection Chart is most appropriate as a summary activity of the play. Students are asked to match the characters from *Macbeth* to the appropriate body part shown in Handout 15. This activity is more than just connecting a character to a specific body part. Rather, students will be creating metaphors, associating specific characters to parts of the human anatomy. Very similar to the synectics from Activities 6 and 7:

> [This] Summarization occurs in more than one place with this technique: first, when students are making analogies, and again, when they are presenting their analogies to others—defending their ideas against critics. It's a highly effective way for them to interact with what they're learning. (Wormeli, 2005, p. 64)

Activity Explained

1. Provide each student with a copy of the chart.
2. Review the meaning of symbols and metaphors, explaining that this activity should reflect symbolic connections between characters and body parts. You may want to create your own example to aid students in their connections.
3. Have students work individually in groups or together to fill in the chart.
4. Alternatively, you may want to have students create posters that visually show their connections between the characters and the body parts.

Handout 15:
Character Body Analogy Connection Chart

Eyes: _____
_____
_____

Brain: _____
_____
_____

Mouth: _____
_____
_____

Heart: _____
_____
_____

Feet: _____
_____
_____

Muscle: _____
_____
_____

Achilles Heel: _____
_____
_____

Activity 13: *Macbeth* RAFT Assignment

A multiple intelligence, role-playing activity, the *Macbeth* RAFT assignment in Handout 16 engages students to think like various characters from the play, with different audiences, different formats, and different time periods. Developed from the work of C. M. Santa (1988), this approach not only aids students in plot analysis of the play, but also leads them to make higher level connections with the text. The students are asked to view the text through four distinct lenses: different roles (R), distinct audiences (A), various formats (F), and many time periods or topics (T).

To use this assignment, students need to select an item from each of the four columns. This differentiated activity engages students by integrating components of the text. Students demonstrate their comprehension and quickly move to higher level thinking in their interpretation and synthesis of the various choices provided. For example, a student may select "Witches" from the role (R) column, "A group of doctors" from the audience (A) column, "A poem," from the format (F) column, and "After the death of Lady Macbeth" in the time period (T) column.

Activity Explained

1. Give each student a copy of the chart.
2. Have students select one choice from each column.
3. Students then generate a scenario applying these four choices as either an alternate writing assignment or a role-play to share with classmates. This opportunity allows different styles of learning to shine; encourage students to make their own choices about which type of product (format) they would like to complete.

Handout 16:
Macbeth RAFT Assignment

ROLE	AUDIENCE	FORMAT	TIME
Macbeth	The Scots	Newspaper account	After the death of Duncan
Lady Macbeth	Children of Scotland	Eulogy	Scotland today
Duncan	Witches	Speech	After the death of Macbeth
Banquo	Citizens of England	Diary entry	After the death of Banquo
Macduff	Mourners at funeral	Letter	After the death of Lady Macbeth
Malcolm	Guests attending coronation ceremony	Obituary	After the death of Macduff's family
Fleance	Servants at Inverness	Song lyrics	Before Macbeth meets Lady Macbeth
The witches	Journalists	Poem	After the coronation of Malcolm
Donalbain	Doctors	Short story	Before Macbeth meets the witches
Lenox	Scottish soldiers	Comic book	Before Macbeth goes to war against Norway
Lady Macduff	Jury	Newspaper editorial	After the Porter awakens
The Porter	Archaeologists	Newscast	One day before Duncan is murdered

Activity 14: *Macbeth* Countdown: 5-4-3-2-1

This activity is a simple countdown that allows students to organize their knowledge about the play. It is useful in allowing the educator to assess the students' level of comprehension and their ability to deduce facts from the Shakespearean language. You may want to use this as a halfway point activity to ensure students are understanding the play.

Activity Explained

1. Introduce this activity by selecting a scene from *Macbeth* and working together as a class.
2. Once students are familiar with the process, divide the class into small groups and have each group work on a different scene to complete the countdown handout.

Handout 17:
Macbeth Countdown: 5-4-3-2-1

ACT_____ SCENE____

5. Write a summary in five sentences.

1.) _____

2.) _____

3.) _____

4.) _____

5.) _____

4. List four important characters.

1.) _____

2.) _____

3.) _____

4.) _____

3. List three quotations from the scene and their significance.

1.) _____

2.) _____

3.) _____

2. Find two literary devices used. Write down the quotations and location. What devices are they?

1.) _____

2.) _____

1. What is one symbol used in the scene?

1.) _____

 Advanced Placement Classroom: Macbeth © Prufrock Press • This page may be photocopied or reproduced with permission for classroom use.

Activity 15: *Macbeth* Question/Answer Relationship (QAR)

Raphael and Au (2005) stated that developing Question and Answer Relationship (QAR) activities in the classroom affects literacy practices and creates a unique, communal classroom language:

> QAR provides a framework that offers teachers a straightforward approach for reading comprehension instruction with the potential of eventually closing the literacy achievement gap. [QAR activities create] a shared language to make visible the largely invisible processes underlying reading and listening comprehension. Thus, QAR, first and foremost, provides teachers and students with a much-needed common language. (p. 208)

This exercise assesses characterization, plot, and theme through higher level questions.

Activity Explained

1. Give each student a copy of Handout 18.
2. Depending on your time frame, consider having students work alone, in pairs, or in small groups.
3. Students then should work to answer each question, using quotes from the text, on a separate piece of paper.
4. In addition, allow students to create their own QAR charts beyond the one provided in Handout 18. Groups can exchange charts and rate the challenge level of their peers' questions.

Handout 18:
Question/Answer Relationship

Right There	Author and You
What are the witches' prophesies in Act 1?	Based on previous discussions about Shakespearean tragedy, how does Shakespeare utilize the Greek term *harmartia* in the play?
What does Macbeth do after he hears the prophesies?	What elements of *Macbeth* foreshadow the murder of Duncan?
Think and Search	**On My Own**
What caused Macbeth to kill Banquo?	Identify a modern example wherein an individual's ambition leads to his or her undoing.
Explain the theme of "vaulting ambition" in the play. Provide two examples where Macbeth gives himself over to his ambition.	If you were a Hollywood producer, what contemporary actors would you cast to portray the lead roles in *Macbeth*?

Activity 16: *Macbeth* Taxonomy Cube

This activity follows Bloom's Revised taxonomy. Based on the work of educational psychologist Benjamin Bloom, who theorized that students think on increasingly hierarchical levels, this cubing activity reflects these ideas. Bloom's Revised taxonomy lays out the structure in a pyramid form beginning with the lowest levels of thinking to the highest, namely the levels of remembering, understanding, applying, analyzing, evaluating, and creating.

Each side of the cube challenges the students at varying levels of comprehension.

Activity Explained

1. Provide each student with a template of the cube, found in Handout 19. Students may want to use this template or make their own cubes.
2. Consider individualizing the task to meet each student's ability or have students roll the cube and work on whatever side faces up.
3. If you prefer for students to answer all of the questions, they can put their answers on the cube, on a larger cube, or on a separate piece of paper, numbering each section of the cube to correspond with their answers.

Handout 19: Bloom's Taxonomy Cube

DIRECTIONS: Please answer the following questions regarding our study of *Macbeth*. After you have completed each of the six boxes, please use scissors and tape to create a six-sided cube to be utilized in class discussions of the play.

Remembering
Please cite all of the witches' prophesies in *Macbeth*.

Applying
Examine the role of Lady Macbeth and her influence on her husband.

Understanding
Why did Macbeth kill King Duncan?

Evaluating
How effective will Malcolm be as the new king of Scotland? Cite examples from the play where you feel that he is the better alternative to Macbeth.

Analyzing
Name and describe two key symbols from the play. Examine the effect of each symbol on the play's outcome.

Creating
Create a new ending to *Macbeth* that explains what you think might have happened had Macbeth never killed Duncan.

Activity 17: *Macbeth* Socratic Seminar

The Socratic Seminar format is used very frequently in the Advanced Placement classroom. For a Socratic Seminar to succeed, the educator needs to prepare a number of higher level, open-ended questions for the class. When utilizing this teaching methodology, the teacher as facilitator/coach metaphor is most appropriate. If you are the type of educator who feels the need to continually "jump in," providing the "correct answer" for your students, then this approach may be a bit challenging. The success or failure of Socratic Seminar relies on the organic nature of the discussion. Having prepared the previous evening's reading, the students should be able to discuss the text in a deeper, more meaningful way. Allow students the intellectual freedom to take chances and challenge one another.

Activity Explained

1. Structurally, there are a number of ways to conduct this type of classroom management strategy. For example, you may have four open-ended questions that you would like to delve into during your class discussion.

2. In order to maintain the appropriate amount of time spent on each question, students should be assigned specific roles that rotate from question to question. One student should be the time keeper, whose task is to manage the appropriate amount of time allotted per question; another should be the scribe, who writes down the student responses; one student should be the question leader, whose task is to call on individual students and keep students on track; and another member of the group should be the summarizer, who reads and summarizes the scribe's copious notes for the large group. However, each student, regardless of the role, should provide his or her own answers to the questions.

3. There is an enormous benefit to having students hear their words shared with the large group. As students share, you can utilize the Socratic Seminar scoring rubric in Handout 20 to maintain a record of positive and negative comments during the seminar.

Name: _____ Date: _____

Handout 20:
Macbeth Socratic Seminar Rubric

Contributions:

1.) States a clear point of view about *Macbeth* _____ x (1)

2.) Provides comments that reflect a high level of academic discourse _____ x (1)

3.) Supports thesis by providing evidence from *Macbeth* _____ x (2)

4.) References another literary work _____ x (1)

5.) Shows evidence of synthesis _____ x (2)

6.) Asks questions of peers _____ x (2)

7.) Rephrases what another student says _____ x (2)

Detriments:

1.) Off-task behavior _____ x (-2)

2.) Calling out without being recognized _____ x (-1)

3.) Random/irrelevant comments _____ x (-1)

4.) Disrespectful comments _____ x (-3)

Contributions: (+) _____

Detriments: (-) _____

Overall Total: (=) _____

 Advanced Placement Classroom: Macbeth © Prufrock Press • This page may be photocopied or reproduced with permission for classroom use.

Activity 18: Will the Real Tanist Please Stand Up?

At the conclusion of *Macbeth*, the audience learns that Malcolm, as established by King Duncan's decision to name his son the Prince of Cumberland, breaks the tradition of the tanistry system. (See Chapter 4 of this text for a further discussion of the idea of tanistry). In this activity, imagine that Macduff, who strolls upon the stage with the head of Macbeth on a pike, wants to become king of Scotland, as does Malcolm's younger brother, Donalbain. Based on the situation and characters of *Macbeth*, determine the rightful leader of the Scottish people. The possible candidates would be Malcolm of the "New Scotland" Party, Macduff of the "Traditional Highland" Party, or Donalbain of the Irish-backed "Kerns and Gallowglass" Party.

Activity Explained

1. This activity can span one class period or an entire week, depending on your timeframe.
2. The students need to select a candidate to support and to create their party's platform. From the discussion, one student in each group will emerge as Malcolm, Macduff, or Donalbain. The objective is for each candidate to create a slogan and persuade the class to elect him or her as ruler of Scotland. Each candidate also must prepare a speech or presentation for election day. Some additional products students may want to create are:
   a. political/stump speeches,
   b. political advertisements,
   c. commercials,
   d. fliers/posters,
   e. buttons, and
   f. T-shirts.

3. Set aside one day as voting day, where each candidate presents his or her case for election as king. Additionally, if students are really engaged in this activity, you may want to allow them several days to "campaign" to their classmates before the voting day. This activity can be enjoyable for all, especially if you set up ballot boxes or voting booths.
4. Someone *must* be elected, which means that negotiation and compromise need to occur. If the students reach a stalemate, remind them that the point of compromise is to "reach across party lines" for the good of Mother Scotland. You also may want to invite an outside class or other teachers/administrators to help ensure one candidate wins.

Activity 19: "Macbeth on Trial": Creative Debate

We live in a litigious society. Corporations and individuals constantly are suing one another for monetary retribution for pain and suffering. Banquo's son, Fleance, is no different. He avers that his father's rights have been violated and he wants retribution, this time monetary compensation, for the pain and suffering he has endured over his father's wrongful death.

Activity Explained

1. Over the course of three class meetings, students will simulate a courtroom setting with Fleance as the plaintiff suing Macbeth for his father's wrongful death and his own pain and suffering that accompanied the murderous ambush.
2. First assign students to roles (see below).
3. Then, provide students with tips for creating each role.
4. Give students at least one class period to create their defense and write questions for the witnesses. Students serving as judge, jury, and in other courtroom roles will want to use this class period to study how the judicial system works and make a plan for how the trial's events will occur based on traditional hearings.
5. Conduct the trial. Have the bailiff serve as time keeper to make sure no one goes over his or her allotted time frame.
6. Once the trial is conducted, have the jury provide its verdict. You may wish to have each student write a briefing for or against the verdict, similar to a Supreme Court briefing after the trial ends.

The following roles will be assigned, and the number in parenthesis denotes the number of students in that specific role. The roles are:

Judge	Prosecution Team (2)
Defense Team (2)	Plaintiff: Fleance
Defendant: Macbeth	Witnesses
Ghost of Banquo	Lady Macbeth
Ross	Lennox
Macduff	Malcolm
Donalbain	Hired Assassins (3)
Witches (3)	Jury (7–12)
Courtroom Stenographer	Bailiff

Some points to ponder for the prosecution team:

- What will your strategy be in the courtroom?

- What information will you provide for the jury to aid in proving your strategy?

- What do you need to say about the defendant that will aid in your monetary pursuit?

- How have Macbeth's actions affected your client?

- Who are the witnesses for the prosecution? Why did you choose those particular individuals?

Some points to ponder for the defense team:

- What is your defense strategy?

- What information will you provide to defend your client?

- How will you be able to prove your client's innocence "beyond a reasonable doubt?"

- What witnesses will you call to disprove the plaintiff's claims?

Some points to ponder for the jurors:

- Listen and take careful notes.

- How will you be able to render a fair and impartial verdict?

Some points to ponder for the witnesses:

- Describe your relationship with the accused.

- What information can you provide about the murder of Banquo?

Some points to ponder for the judge:

- Be sure to familiarize yourself with legal terminology (i.e., objection, sustained, overruled, contempt of court, and wrongful death).

- How will you charge the jury with its responsibilities?

- How will you maintain order in the court?

Activity 20: *Macbeth* Soundtrack Assignment

Music selections that accompany movies and television shows provide the audience with a deeper insight into the emotional development of characters. Whether happy or sad, a musical soundtrack offers the audience with an audio progression that adds a great deal to the viewing experience. Think of some of your favorite movies and the music that has accompanied specific scenes in the movie. Did the music scare you? Did it make you cry? Did it make you laugh?

As you conclude your examination of one of Shakespeare's most famous plays with your students, think about the varied interpretations of Shakespeare's words. One area that Shakespeare forgot to include, however, was a soundtrack for his play. Provide a similar introduction to this one to the students. Then, ask students: What songs would you place in the play to describe Macbeth's development as a character from the beginning of the play to its conclusion? Their task in this assignment will be to create a soundtrack to the play to share with their classmates. Each student also will be responsible to creating a brief presentation of why each song was chosen.

Activity Explained

1. Have students pick groups in which to work. (No more than three members per group. You may want to assign groups.)
2. To complete this task, students will need to have:
   a. Three musical selections that reflect the different stages of Macbeth's progression or decline throughout the play. See Handout 21 for the "Describing Macbeth's Change in Character" graphic organizer. Students may record/perform their own music and lyrics if they wish. You also may want to have the librarian provide a selection of CDs appropriate for the classroom for students to use.
   b. Three typed one-page connections in MLA format to the music and the play. Students must connect specific line citations from the play to their analysis of the music lyrics. These documents provide a base for the student presentations.
   c. A packet of song lyrics for each member of the class to read and ponder.
   d. A burned CD to listen to in class, submitted after the student presentation.
   e. An artistic CD cover that reflects the overall theme of the soundtrack.

3. Give students the *Macbeth* Creative CD Rubric in Handout 22. You may want to offer time before and after school for students to work on classroom or library computers to create their soundtracks. The school librarian or technology coordinator should be able to show you the music and CD burning software available at your school, and possibly provide you with a CD for each group to use. This option allows students without access to computers and software to complete the assignment.

4. Once students have completed their soundtracks, they should prepare a brief presentation that explains why they chose each song and share their album artwork with the class. Students will be judged by their peers using Handout 23.

Handout 21:
Describing Macbeth's Change in Character

The Beginning of the Play	The Middle of the Play	The Conclusion of the Play
Words to Describe Macbeth:	Words to Describe Macbeth:	Words to Describe Macbeth:

Name: _____ Date: _____

Handout 22:
Macbeth Creative CD Rubric

Musical Selection #1 /35 points

Appropriateness of music and lyrics (15 points):

Connection to *Macbeth* (20 points):

Musical Selection #2 /35 points

Appropriateness of music and lyrics (15 points):

Connection to *Macbeth* (20 points):

Musical Selection #3 /35 points

Appropriateness of music and lyrics (15 points):

Connection to *Macbeth* (20 points):

CD Cover: Artistic representation of the musical soundtrack /15 points

---

Presentation Style: /5 points
    A. Clarity, volume
    B. Eye contact
    C. Enthusiasm

Peer Evaluation: /5 points

Total: _____ /130 points

Group Members:

Handout 23:
Peer Evaluations for Soundtrack Presentation

Group #
Presentation Style: /5 pts.
A. Clarity, volume
B. Eye contact
C. Enthusiasm

COMMENTS:

Group #
Presentation Style: /5 pts.
A. Clarity, volume
B. Eye contact
C. Enthusiasm

COMMENTS:

Group #
Presentation Style: /5 pts.
A. Clarity, volume
B. Eye contact
C. Enthusiasm

COMMENTS:

Group #
Presentation Style: /5 pts.
A. Clarity, volume
B. Eye contact
C. Enthusiasm

COMMENTS:

Additional Materials for the Classroom: Lesson Ideas, Guided Questions, Key Quotations, and Facts Regarding *Macbeth*

More Lesson Ideas

- Find difficult vocabulary words and create your own definitions and parts of speech. Use the newly defined words in a sentence or a paragraph.

- Research the history of James I. How did he become king? Comment on the role of other major historical figures of the time: Henry VIII, Elizabeth I, and Mary, Queen of Scots.

- Panel discussion: Make a case for or against Macduff's claim to the throne in lieu of Malcolm. Have two teams with a research group supporting them.

- Create a 5-minute *Macbeth* and act it out.

- Film a 5-minute claymation *Macbeth*.

- Research the humors: sanguinity (blood), choleric, bile (yellow, black), phlegmatic. Analyze the key characters and consider which humor would apply. Use a color chart to assess their mood changes throughout the play.

- Compose a short play that concentrates on the lives of the following characters before the play begins: Macbeth, Lady Macbeth, Macduff, Banquo, Lennox, Ross, and Malcolm.

- Construct the Globe Theatre.

❧ Review the tradition of primogeniture. Compare Duncan's transfer of power to Malcolm to King Hussein of Jordan's controversial decision in 1999 and to King David's decision to select Solomon in biblical times.

❧ Using food as the reason, compose a humorous piece explaining why Macbeth decides to be the "harbinger" and ride ahead of King Duncan in Act I, scene iv to see his wife.

❧ Reenact a social event where people say one thing but mean another.

❧ Pretend you are a newspaper reporter who stealthily attended the banquet where Macbeth sees a ghost. Compose a news article explaining the event.

❧ Portray the closing scene with Macduff, Malcolm, and the Scottish thanes in two ways: one with great enthusiasm, the other with a weariness that acknowledges but does not endorse Malcolm as the new king.

Guided Questions

The guided study questions are structured sequentially to help you determine how well your students comprehend the material. Students may answer these questions for homework and/or classroom discussion. Remind students to cite textual evidence when answering.

Act I

1. Describe the setting of the opening scene. What mood is evoked?
2. Why do the witches say, "Fair is foul and fair is foul"?
3. What does the way Macbeth defeated Macdonwald tell the reader about Macbeth?
4. Identify the similes spoken by the captain in scene ii.
5. Describe the details in the battle against Sweno, the King of Norway.
6. Which word in scene ii did not exist in the historical Macbeth's time?
7. Locate contradictory phrasing in other acts. Note how they contribute to the ambiguity of the play.
8. Analyze Macbeth's first spoken words in the play in scene iii, line 39. Discuss their meaning on a connotative and denotative level.
9. In scene iii, list the predictions the witches make for Macbeth and for Banquo.
10. Shakespeare initiates a series of clothing references throughout the play. Explain the "borrowed robes" reference (I. iii. 115). Also, keep a record of clothing metaphors and interpret their meaning. Note who is speak-

ing and explain the circumstances surrounding the imagery. For example, Banquo says "strange garments" (I. iii. 161) a few lines later.

11. Why is Duncan's appointment of Malcolm as Prince of Cumberland in scene iv important as a plot device and a historical footnote?

12. In scene v, why does Lady Macbeth call on evil spirits?

13. What is Lady Macbeth's main concern about her husband?

14. Appearance/reality is a key motif in the play. Cite the lines in scenes v–vi that reveal this motif.

15. In the opening soliloquy of scene vii, Macbeth lists three reasons for opposing the murder of Duncan. What are they? What does Macbeth determine to be his sole justification for killing the king?

16. How does Lady Macbeth convince her husband to kill Duncan? Why are her arguments effective?

Act II

1. What two motifs does Banquo introduce in scene i? What does Banquo reveal about his state of mind in lines 5–11? How are Banquo and Macbeth's behavior similar in the opening of this act? What does the dagger hallucination tell the reader about Macbeth's state of mind?

2. In scene ii, explain why Lady Macbeth does not kill Duncan. Compare her behavior in this scene to your first impression of her in Act I.

3. Why is Macbeth unable to say "amen" (II. ii. 37–44)?

4. Argue the significance of the porter scene from the following two different perspectives: first, look at it from a comic relief point of view; second, argue its importance as a microcosm of the murder scene that just occurred in the castle.

5. From the point that Macduff enters into Duncan's chamber to the end of the scene iii, identify the images used by the people in the castle to express chaos.

6. What is ironic about Macbeth's speech scene iii, lines 107–112?

7. Why do Malcolm and Donalbain decide to flee Scotland?

8. Why do all of the unnatural events discussed in scene iv by the Old Man and Ross occur?

Act III

1. Explain how Macbeth's inviting Banquo to the feast is an example of foreshadowing.

2. How does Macbeth influence the murderers to do his biding? What is ironic about Macbeth's means of persuasion in scene i, lines 95–101?

3. Assess the state of the Macbeths' marriage in scene ii. Provide lines and details that describe their relationship.

4. What is the turning point of the play?

5. Irony is pervasive in this play. In scene iv, Macbeth tells the guests at the banquet, "You know your own degrees; sit down" (III. iv. 1). What is ironic about Macbeth's remark?

6. Explain the significance of the ghost's decision to sit in Macbeth's chair.

7. What does Macbeth mean when he says, "I keep a servant fee'd" (III. iv. 164).

8. Review the remarks made about Macduff in scene vi. Based on what is said, create a profile of Macduff. Predict the role Macduff will have in Acts IV and V.

Act IV

1. Looking at the events in scene i, create an argument that favors or opposes any chance that Macbeth can redeem himself. Cite lines to support your thesis.

2. What do the spirits tell Macbeth?

3. Lennox says he did not see the witches. Are the witches real or, like the dagger and Banquo's ghost, a figment of Macbeth's imagination?

4. In scene ii, explain Macbeth's reasons for attacking Macduff's castle.

5. Cite the lines in scene iii that show Malcolm testing Macduff's loyalty.

6. Review the kingly graces listed by Malcolm in scene iii, lines 107–110. Are these qualities applicable to leaders today?

7. Why does Macduff banish himself from Scotland in scene iii, lines 129–132?

8. List the imagery conveyed in Ross' words as he informs Macduff of his family's death. Indicate the verbs and adjectives.

9. Compare/contrast Malcolm's and Macduff's reactions to Ross' news in scene iii.

Act V

1. Why is Lady Macbeth sleepwalking?

2. Compare Lady Macbeth's attitude about the blood on her hands after the king's murder to the blood on her hands in scene i.

3. The gentlewoman and doctor express sympathy toward Lady Macbeth. Do you?

4. In scene ii, cite the imagery Caithness and Angus employ to describe Macbeth's leadership.

5. Why does Macbeth dismiss the "reports" (V. iii. 1)?
6. Seyton is a homonym for Satan. Why did Shakespeare give Macbeth's ally this name?
7. How does the "Tomorrow" speech (V. v. 22–31) reflect Macbeth's point of view?
8. Why does Macduff refuse to fight "wretched kerns" (V. vii. 22)?
9. How is Macduff considered, "none of woman born" (IV. i. 91)?
10. How does Malcolm reward his loyal followers in his closing speech?

Key Quotations

In every Shakespeare play there are memorable lines. These quotations convey characterizations pertinent to the plot structure of the particular play. In addition, there is a universal aspect about these quotations that, like Shakespeare himself, goes beyond their time and the plot's immediacy. Enjoy them for their phrasing, their timelessness, and the imagery they evoke. Ask students to comment on them or to recite them aloud.

Select a few of the quotations listed below and ask students to interpret their importance, or have students choose a quotation that they found to be meaningful to the play or to their own lives.

Act I

"Fair is foul, and foul is fair" (I. i. 12): The witches

Spoken by the witches, this quotation, introducing a paradox at the beginning of the play, immediately establishes a motif of appearance and reality. Macbeth echoes this sentiment in Act I, scene iii, line 39. Shakespeare links the characters of the witches and Macbeth, which is particularly poignant, because Macbeth is a hero, fighting bravely for his king and Scotland, and the witches are instruments of evil.

"The Thane of Cawdor lives / A prosperous gentleman, and to be king / Stands not within the prospect of belief" (I. iii. 75–77): Macbeth

Macbeth and Banquo return from the war and come upon the witches on the heath. The strange beings predict that Macbeth will be king and Banquo will be the father of a line of kings. Both are war heroes and, as the quotation indicates, Macbeth is a loyal noble proclaiming that being king is not feasible. A page later, Ross and Angus arrive to confirm part of the witches' predictions in Act I, scene iii, lines 109–112. Macbeth, already Thane of Glamis, adds the title of Thane of Cawdor.

"But 'tis strange. / And oftentimes, to win us to our harm, / The instruments of darkness tell us truths, / Win us with honest trifles" (I. iii. 134–138): Banquo

Talking to Macbeth, Banquo offers advice about these strange beings that appeared in front of them on their return from battle. He warns Macbeth not to listen to what these creatures are saying. Frequently, those who wish us harm entice us with tiny truths only to ruin us in realms that are more important. Banquo proves to be honest and forthright. He tells the audience that he will not be duped by supposedly sweet offerings. In essence, Banquo gives the witches the same credence one may give a fortune-teller. Macbeth, however, is intrigued, weighing the prospect of being king in his mind. Review the aside that follows Banquo's quotation.

To modernize this quotation, parallel this speech to the possible influence of peer pressure, either positive or negative, in the areas of drugs, sex, and underage drinking. Banquo understands that short-term gain sometimes results in long-term loss. Macbeth appears unable to comprehend this concept.

"If chance will have me king, why, chance may / crown me / Without my stir." (I. iii. 157–159): Macbeth

As Macbeth ruminates about his new honor and the uncanny nature of the witches, he considers a course of action that is critical to his future success or failure. If the witches speak the truth, then he really does not have to take any action. Fate will draw him to the crown as correctly as it predicted his position as Thane of Cawdor. Macbeth, as the viewer/reader quickly learns, will not choose fate's path.

"There's no art / To find the mind's construction in the face. / He was a gentleman on whom I built / An absolute trust" (I. iv. 13–16): Duncan

Shakespeare establishes the irony of Duncan's trusting remark by replacing one traitorous Thane of Cawdor with another. Duncan's naiveté is on display when Macbeth enters after the word "trust." Duncan is saying that one's thoughts cannot be detected by one's facial expressions. Duncan dismisses the flawed practice of physiognomy or, more likely, criticizes his own poor judgment skills, observing how Cawdor's traitorous behavior eluded him. Lady Macbeth will, conversely, lend credence to the ease with which one may read Macbeth's thoughts just by looking at his expressions in Act I, scene v, lines 73–74.

"Hie thee hither, / That I may pour my spirits in thine ear / And chastise with the valor of my tongue / All that impedes thee" (I. v. 28–31): Lady Macbeth

Having read the letter from her husband, Lady Macbeth worries that her husband is not ambitious enough to take the necessary steps required to be king. She, of course, knows what to do and wishes that Macbeth would hurry home, so that she may persuade him to act accordingly. Her ruthlessness is present immediately.

"Come, you spirits / That tend on mortal thoughts, unsex me here, / And fill me from the crown to the toe top-full / Of direst cruelty" (I. v. 47–50): Lady Macbeth

These lines are part of a larger soliloquy that defines Lady Macbeth's character. She prays to evil spirits to make her genderless (or more specifically like a man), so that she may act without the pangs of conscience. Coleridge writes, "Shakespeare's characters are the representatives of the interior nature of humanity, in which some element has become so predominant as to destroy the health of the mind" (as cited in Snyder, 1923, p. 25). The destructive element for her is an inability to suppress guilt.

Lady Macbeth's actions are indirect rather than direct. She persuades her husband to act, and, as happens later in the play, she deflects attention away from his behavior. To achieve her goal, she requires her husband to commit regicide. Her invitation to evil, she believes, will allow her to function free from moral constraints. As the audience sees in Act V, scene i, Lady Macbeth fails to suppress her conscience.

"Look like th' innocent / flower, / But be the serpent under 't" (I. v. 76–78): Lady Macbeth

Lady Macbeth warns her husband that his face must disguise his true intent. The king is arriving and Macbeth's mask of loyalty must be in tact. King Duncan at the beginning of the next scene quickly duplicates this line, establishing the appearance/reality motif so prominently developed in this play when he observes how sensuous Macbeth's castle appears.

"I have no spur / To prick the sides of my intent, but only / Vaulting ambition, which o'erleaps itself / And falls on th' other—" (I. vii. 25–28): Macbeth

Duncan is visiting and Macbeth leaves the table to ruminate about killing his king. Reviewing all his reasons, he concludes that his only justification is ambition. He decides to back away from the plan until Lady Macbeth comes into the room and persuades him to kill Duncan by questioning his manliness. The imagery conveyed in the quotation is of a rider who leaps too far while jumping into a saddle, only to tumble over the other side.

"I have given suck, and know / How tender 'tis to love the babe that milks me." (I. vii. 62–63): Lady Macbeth

This line follows her disgust at her husband's vacillation. As far as she is concerned, Duncan's presence offers the perfect opportunity to strike. This line reveals that she had a child in a previous marriage, but the Macbeths are childless. The intensity of the line and the monstrous content of the speech reveal a person completely outside the moral sphere of humanity.

Coleridge, who had difficulty conceptualizing that any woman could even think this way about a nursing infant, said:

> Lady Macbeth, acting in a merciless and unwomanly nature, brings to Macbeth a most solemn enforcement of the solemnity of his promise to undertake the plot against Duncan. Had she so sworn, she would have done that which was most horrible to her feelings, rather than break the oath. (as cited in Barnet, 1956, p. 18)

Citing such a horrific example as a means of persuading her husband to commit a monstrous act immures Lady Macbeth from the consequences to such an extent that the viewer/reader will have difficulty comprehending such barbarity.

Continue to analyze Lady Macbeth's speeches. Have the students maintain a psychological profile of her character throughout the play in a journal.

Act II

"Is this a dagger which I see before me, / The handle toward my hand?" (II. i. 44–45): Macbeth

Macbeth waits for the bell to signal him to action. His hallucination grows more graphic with its imagery of blood on the blade and handle. His dagger hallucination weaves fantasy with reality revealing how wearing this action is on him. Not that long ago, Macbeth was receiving well-earned accolades for his bravery. Now, he stands alone, waiting to murder his sleeping king. Shakespeare alludes to *The Rape of Lucrece* in Macbeth's soliloquy when he describes Tarquin, the rapist, moving toward his victim.

"I laid their daggers ready; / He could not miss 'em. Had he not resembled / My father as he slept, I had done 't" (II. ii. 15–17): Lady Macbeth

The plan, as devised by Lady Macbeth, is to get the guards drunk, stab Duncan with their weapons, and return the weapons to the drugged guards. Lady Macbeth reveals that she does have a standard of decency, albeit relatively low. As noted earlier, Lady Macbeth functions as her husband's evil advisor. Her murderous plan securely in place, Macbeth puts it into effect.

"Methought I heard a voice cry 'Sleep no more! / Macbeth does murder sleep'" (II. ii. 47–48): Macbeth

Sleep is another key motif in this play. There is a zombie-like quality to Macbeth immediately after the murder. He has no peace and certainly no joy in what he just did. The dialogue with Lady Macbeth details the consequence of his crime—murdering sleep. He divides himself into three noting that "'Glamis hath murdered sleep, and therefore / Cawdor / Shall sleep no more. Macbeth shall sleep no more'" (II. ii. 55–57). The voice is described as external with the punishment being internal, and the outcome for Macbeth is sleeplessness. Have your students throughout the play identify the physical and emotional manifestations of Macbeth's "murdering sleep."

Shakespeare's adaptation of Holinshed's history is evident in the voices Macbeth hears. Holinshed described:

> [...] a mysterious voice after King Kenneth had slain his nephew: A voice was heard as he was in bed in the night time to take his rest, [...] 'Thinke not Kenneth that the wicked slaughter of Malcolme Duffe by thee contrived, is kept secret from the knowledge of the eternall God. (Muir, 1992, p. 166)

"Give me the daggers. The sleeping and the dead / Are but as pictures. 'Tis the eye of childhood / That fears a painted devil." (II. ii. 69–71): Lady Macbeth

Showing military precision and logic, Lady Macbeth takes the bloody daggers from her husband and places them on the guards, according to the plan she devised. Macbeth appears stunned to inaction, so his wife must act. The warrior, who doubled his efforts while responding so bravely to the rebels and to Norway, instantly regrets his murderous actions and cannot move.

"Had I but died an hour before this chance, / I had lived a blessèd time" (II. iii. 107–108): Macbeth

While Macbeth obsequiously plays to the shocked nobility, he unintentionally tells the truth. Had he died an hour earlier, he would have been honored forever as a Scottish hero. Tales about his bravery would have been sung throughout the kingdom. Instead his reputation will be just the opposite. Macbeth speaks poetically about Duncan's death while Macduff bluntly tells Donalbain that his father is murdered. Shortly after his speech, Macbeth confesses to killing the guards after he sees the bloody weapons lying near them. His love for King Duncan, he says, forced him to act against these apparent murderers.

This scene marks a split between his wife and him. Killing the guards was not part of the original plan, so he acts independently. Lady Macbeth faints. Is her behavior a ploy or a sincere reaction to a change in circumstances?

"Where we are, / There's daggers in men's smiles. The near in blood, / The nearer bloody" (II. iii. 164–166): Donalbain

Because of the danger to their lives, Malcolm and Donalbain decide to leave Scotland and flee to England and Ireland, respectively. Donalbain observes that the assassin is close by and most likely is the one who fawns over them the most.

His remarks continue the appearance/reality motif. The reader/viewer should keep in mind that Malcolm was named Prince of Cumberland, and his first act as the heir-apparent to the throne is to flee the castle.

"No, cousin, I'll to Fife" (II. iv. 50): Macduff

Macduff, the Thane of Fife, very clearly and publicly disavows any hint of support for Macbeth's coronation at Scone. His decision not to attend the ceremonies is a complete repudiation of Macbeth. He simply chooses to go home. Macbeth, of course, is very aware of who is and who is not in attendance. For Macduff the path to the crown wound too smoothly. Beginning with his disapproval of the guards' killing on the night of Duncan's murder, Macduff has chosen to be an enemy of the new king.

Act III

"To be thus is nothing, / But to be safely thus." (III. i. 52–53): Macbeth

After urging Banquo to be on time for the evening's banquet, Macbeth, in soliloquy, assesses his current situation. To be the king, "thus," is to be nothing if he cannot provide for his own safety. Reviewing Banquo's questions to the witches, he determines that Banquo is a threat. Why else would Banquo want to know his own future when questioning the witches? Of course, Macbeth fails to see that he has created a world that lacks order and, therefore, safety. Without children, Macbeth concludes that Banquo must be killed to ensure that his efforts, Macbeth's murder of Duncan and his crowning at Scone, were not in vain. After all, he says, he did not go through with the murderous plan just to benefit Banquo and his descendants.

"Better be with the dead, / Whom we, to gain our peace, have sent to peace, / Than on the torture of the mind to lie / In restless ecstasy" (III. ii. 22–25): Macbeth

The lack of sleep gets its full airing as Macbeth enviously compares the murdered Duncan's peaceful sleep to his own nightly affliction. Macbeth reports that he and his wife have nightmares every night. To counter her husband's distress, Lady Macbeth looks forward to the feast that evening and gently warns Macbeth to appear jovial. Meeting with the murderers and setting up the ambush of Banquo and Fleance, Macbeth reveals the growing schism between him and his wife. Macbeth acts independently, referring to Banquo vaguely.

"This is the very painting of your fear. / This is the air-drawn dagger which you said / Led you to Duncan" (III. iv. 74–76): Lady Macbeth

Lady Macbeth's quotation tells us that her husband discussed the first hallucination with her, an open discussion that rarely appears to occur between them anymore. Her remark occurs after Macbeth publicly screams at Banquo's ghost, a sight only he sees. She draws him aside and asks if he is a man, an accusation last heard before Duncan's death. She covers for his outburst by revealing that this behavior has been an affliction from his youth. The festivities are ruined and the thanes leave.

"The time has been / That, when the brains were out, the man would die, / And there an end" (III. iv. 94–96): Macbeth

Macbeth's outcry occurs in between ghost appearances and exits. He notes that even the dead do not follow the course of nature. Tying in with the viewpoint of universal balance promulgated in Elizabethan and Jacobean England, Macbeth sees no link between these strange occurrences and his crime of regicide. In Scotland under his reign, nature is out of balance and one consequence is that the dead "push us from our stools" (III. iv. 98).

"It will have blood, they say; blood will have blood. / Stones have been known to move, and trees to speak" (III. iv. 151–153): Macbeth

Macbeth expresses his fear of detection here. "It" refers to Banquo's murder. The imagery of moving stones originates with a Druid test to determine guilt or innocence of a traitor who may have acted without any witnesses. Gigantic stones were placed on top of each other, centuries earlier. The slightest touch would cause them to vibrate, but not in a dangerous way. In front of a judge, the accused would touch the stone. If it vibrated, the accused were innocent. Believing the stone to possess divine power, the guilty would confess in awe of its weighty mass (Wylie, 1887).

"And I do think / That had he Duncan's sons under his key / (As, an 't please heaven, he shall not) they should / find / What 'twere to kill a father." (III. vi. 18–22): Lennox

Indicating a weakening of support among the Scottish thanes, Lennox's conversation with another noble sarcastically centers on the apparent preponderance of patricides occurring in Scotland. He notes Malcolm's and Donalbain's fleeing after Duncan's death and Fleance's running away after Banquo's sudden death, too. The atmosphere under Macbeth's regime requires quiet talk because spies are everywhere.

Lennox recalls Macbeth's pious response to Duncan's drunken guards considering Macbeth's action "nobly done . . . and wisely, too" (III. vi. 15). Lennox prays that Macbeth never captures Malcolm, Donalbain, and Fleance. The conversation shifts to Macduff, who declined an invitation to join Macbeth. The Lord indicates that Macduff is seeking aid from Northumberland and Siward in England. Both nobles hope that Scotland returns to a country that is at peace. The message underlying that wish can only occur with Macbeth's demise.

Act IV

"Double, double toil and trouble; / Fire burn, and cauldron bubble." (IV. i. 10–11): Witches

There is a mix of the horrible and the comedic in this scene. The witches intend to continue making trouble for Macbeth. At the same time, audiences are fascinated with the ingredients stirred into the cauldron. The items range from the disgusting to the fantastic. After each witch tosses in her special ingredients, all three chant the "double, double" couplet.

The witches certainly captivated the audiences in Shakespeare's time. To differentiate these beings from royalty, Shakespeare changed the rhythmic structure of their speech. Instead of the standard iambic pentameter, 10 syllables with the stress on the second one, the witches speak in trochaic tetrameter, with a stress on the first syllable followed by an unstressed syllable. The prosodic structure of the individual witch's chants that follow is written in a catalectic or truncated form of trochaic tetrameter with a line missing a syllable in the last foot (Baer, 2006). When counting the syllables, one will observe seven syllables in the line instead of eight.

"Infected be the air whereon they ride, / And damned all those that trust them!" (IV. i. 157–158): Macbeth

After meeting with the witches and hearing what he believes are positive predictions from the evil spirits, Macbeth finds out that Banquo's family will reign for what appears to be eternity. The last image is a group of kings with a bloody Banquo, holding a mirror, standing at the end of the line, which symbolizes more and more descendants to come. After the witches vanish and Lennox appears, Macbeth utters the above quotation. Of course, the irony is that Macbeth just cursed himself. Lennox also reports that Macduff has fled to England. Ordering an attack on Macduff's castle, Macbeth mandates that no one survives.

"I am not to you known, / Though in your state of honor I am perfect." (IV. ii. 71–72): Messenger

Following Ross, the mysterious messenger warns Lady Macduff and her son to escape from their castle immediately. Revealing that he or she knows the noble rank of Lady Macduff, this person has specific information that their lives are in jeopardy. Who is this person? A spy whom Macbeth placed in the castle who suddenly turned against Macbeth? Lady Macbeth, who has been left out of the decision-making process for some time now? An unnamed noble who is working in concert with Ross to reinforce the message that the castle is about to be attacked? Consider the options and decide who this person may be. As we soon see, murderers appear, and Macduff's family is doomed.

"Each new morn / New widows howl, new orphans cry, new sorrows / Strike heaven on the face" (IV. iii. 5–7): Macduff

In this scene, Macduff sadly describes the state of Scotland to Malcolm. Earlier in the play, Duncan named Malcolm Prince of Cumberland, making him the heir to the throne. Fleeing to England after his father's murder, Malcolm receives reports from various contacts about the state of Scotland under Macbeth's murderous regime. Some visitors have been sycophants of Macbeth hoping to lure Malcolm back to Scotland.

There is dramatic irony in this quotation because the audience knows about the fate of Macduff's family from the previous scene. Another part of the quotation is "new sorrows / Strike heaven on the face, that it resounds / As if it felt with Scotland" (IV. iii. 6–8). Adding to the dramatic irony, Macduff, unaware of his family's situation, is speaking generally about the state of Scotland.

"Such welcome and unwelcome things at once / 'Tis hard to reconcile." (IV. iii. 157–158): Macduff

Malcolm engages Macduff in a lengthy conversation where Malcolm pretends to be worse than Macbeth. Malcolm lists the kingly virtues and repudiates all of them as a way to assess Macduff's response. Macduff banishes himself from Scotland, saying, "These evils thou repeat'st upon thyself / Hath banished me from Scotland" (IV. iii. 130–131).

Sensing sincerity, Malcolm confesses that he was speaking falsely because Macbeth has sent people like Macduff to trick him into returning home. After hearing a litany of behaviors that sound worse than Macbeth, Macduff sees little hope for Scotland's future, banishing himself. To find out that Malcolm was just testing him puts Macduff through a rollercoaster of emotions, which prompts the aforementioned quotation. Sadly, Macduff finds out the truth about his family soon after this conversation.

"Alas, poor country, / Almost afraid to know itself [. . .] / Where sighs and groans and shrieks that rent the air / Are made, not marked" (IV. iii. 189–194): Ross

Playing the role of messenger, Ross reports the horror that is now Scotland. Pay attention to the nouns and verbs incorporated into Ross' remarks. There is an onomatopoeic quality to the description with words like sighs, groans, shrieks, and rent. Later, adding even more sound imagery, Ross refers to a "dead man's knell" (IV. iii. 195), or the tolling of the bells symbolizing death.

"He has no children" (IV. iii. 255): Macduff

After hearing Ross deliver the news of his family's murder by Macbeth, Macduff responds to Malcolm's advice about seeking revenge. Muir indicates three possible explanations for the unidentified pronoun "he." First, it could refer to Malcolm, who, having no children, would otherwise propose different advice to someone who was informed moments ago that his family is dead. Another interpretation is that the reference is to Macduff, who has no children of his own. Macduff cannot deliver an equal response to Macbeth. However, the reasoning is, had he had children, Macbeth never would have committed such a heinous act (Muir, 1992).

Act V

"Out, damned spot, out, I say! One. Two. / Why then, 'tis time to do 't." (V. i. 37–38): Lady Macbeth

This very famous quotation from the play encapsulates the range of character traits demonstrated by Lady Macbeth throughout the plot. After Duncan's murder, Lady Macbeth calms her husband by simply noting that a bowl of water will clean the blood from his hands. When Macbeth kills the guards, Lady Macbeth faints, drawing attention away from his act momentarily. When Macbeth sees Banquo's ghost occupying his chair, Lady Macbeth, once again, improvises, telling the nobles in attendance that her husband has had an affliction since childhood that occasionally surfaces. What we learn in this scene is that she cannot ward away the demons that haunt her. Slowly, over time, the decisions that the Macbeths make wear away the cold sheen shrouding her conscience. Now that regret or remorse seeps in, she cannot stop it. Furthermore, the lack of restful sleep is exacerbating her condition.

Lady Macbeth's sleepwalking is a manifestation of her guilty conscience. She hallucinates, seeing bloodspots on her hands. The counting in the quotation, "One. Two." could be the hour in which the murder of Duncan took place. Another possibility is that she is counting the spots on her hand that will not wash off.

"But for certain / He cannot buckle his distempered cause / Within the belt of rule" (V. ii. 16–18): Caithness
"Now does he feel his title / Hang loose about him, like a giant's robe / Upon a dwarfish thief." (V. ii. 23–25): Angus

The two quotations by different Scottish nobles are bundled together because of Shakespeare's clothing imagery. The first is a metaphor and the second is a simile. Both use clothing to comment on Macbeth's waning power. As his allies leave him and join forces with the English, Macbeth's power diminishes and his future appears bleak.

The first reference indicates that Macbeth's kingdom is ill and so swollen with corruption that Macbeth cannot contain or control it anymore. Angus, another Scottish noble, observes that the dignity associated with the crown is ill suited for Macbeth. By using the word *thief*, Shakespeare alludes to the consensus of the Scottish nobility toward Macbeth. Angus and Caithness function as a Greek chorus, informing the audience of the plot and commenting on the protagonist.

"Those he commands move only in command, / Nothing in love."
(V. ii. 22–23): Angus

Angus, a Scottish noble, remarks that those unfortunate souls fighting for Macbeth do so only under the threat of punishment. Very few believe in Macbeth's cause. Perhaps some students will research modern or historical examples that parallel Angus' comment.

"And that which should accompany old age, / As honor, love, obedience, troops of friends, / I must not look to have" (V. iii. 28–30): Macbeth

Despair filters its way into Macbeth's voice as he sees his kingdom fall apart. His vision of a glorious life as king has fallen far short of his initial expectation. His forces are deserting him and the English forces are close to the gate of his castle. Sycophants that hope to gain approval for what they say more than what they mean surround Macbeth. Those around him do not act out of loyalty, just opportunity.

"Both more and less have given him the revolt, / And none serve him but constrainèd things / Whose hearts are absent too." (V. iv. 16–18): Malcolm

Having approached Birnam Wood, Malcolm remarks that he heard that both nobles and commoners are abandoning Macbeth's army. Having little military experience, Malcolm bases his assessment on rumors. Macduff quickly says, "Let our just censures / Attend the true event" (V. iv. 19–20). He means that judgment should be reserved until their forces confront Macbeth's. Essentially, Macduff says to wait and see whether Macbeth's forces are diminished.

"Tomorrow and tomorrow and tomorrow / Creeps in this petty pace from day to day . . . " (V. v. 22–31): Macbeth

This long quotation by Macbeth is discussed in Chapter 2. The key is to focus on characterization and setting. Analyze how the circumstances result in the viewpoint that Macbeth promulgates. Look at whether Macbeth's change over the course of the play is a matter of free will or fate. This speech captures his despair for his actions and his view that life, particularly his life, is insignificant.

Consider the following discussion question: Throughout the play is Macbeth guided by fate or free will? Process the question in a small-group discussion and/or an essay.

"And let the angel whom thou still hast served / Tell thee Macduff was from his mother's womb / Untimely ripped." (V. viii. 18–20): Macduff

Macduff reveals that a doctor performed a Caesarian section on his mother so that he would live. Poor medical conditions resulted in Macduff's mother's death. The second apparition says, "Laugh to scorn / The power of man, for none of woman born / Shall harm Macbeth" (IV. i. 90–92). The spirits confuse Macbeth. He interprets the prediction literally, considering only the reality that everyone is born of woman. He never knows whether they were speaking denotatively or connotatively. Unfortunately, Macbeth knows now.

"And be these juggling fiends no more believed / That palter with us in a double sense" (V. viii. 23–24): Macbeth

After all the destruction he caused, Macbeth finally realizes that he was tricked. "Double sense" continues the appearance/reality motif. Macbeth was two-faced when he welcomes King Duncan into his home, while planning his murder. His former friend, Banquo, himself a victim of Macbeth's treachery, warns him that the witches entice their victims with small tidbits, only to deceive them when the stakes are more important.

Macbeth yields to Macduff at this point, acknowledging that too much of Macduff's family's blood is on his conscience already. After Macduff paints a picture of what his life will be like under King Malcolm's rule, Macbeth decides to fight to the death. He yells, "Lay on, Macduff, / And damned be him that first cries 'Hold! Enough!'" (V. viii. 38–39).

"My thanes and / kinsmen, / Henceforth be earls, the first that ever Scotland / In such an honor named." (V. viii. 74–76): Malcolm

Holinshed reports that after Malcolm's coronation at Scone on April 25, 1057, the newly crowned monarch rewarded those Scottish thanes who supported him against Macbeth with land and entitlements (Hosley, 1968). Among the thanes who became earls were Fife, Menteith, Lennox, Caithness, Ross, and Angus (Muir, 1992). Malcolm's changing the title of thanes to earls shifted a time-honored Scottish custom toward a more civilized English tradition. This attempt to unite the Scottish and English crowns would have greatly pleased the Scottish/English monarch James I of England.

Fun Facts About *Macbeth:* Did You Know . . . ?

- James I composed an essay entitled, "A Counterblast to Tobacco," that denounced smoking.

- *Macbeth* was Abraham Lincoln's favorite Shakespeare play, and ironically, John Wilkes Booth once portrayed Macbeth.

- Macbeth's real name is Mac Bethad mac Findláich. He was a true 11th-century Scottish king.

- Lady Macbeth, the granddaughter of Kenneth III, is named Gruoch.

- Macbeth was killed in battle in 1057, by Malcolm Canmore, the future Malcolm III.

- Macbeth excludes any reference to Banquo in the letter to his wife, pretending that he, alone, met with the witches.

- The publication, *A Treaty of Equivocation* by Reverend Henry Garnet, S. J., which "supports the morality of giving misleading answers under oath" (Greenblatt, 2004, p. 336), led to his execution in the Gunpowder Plot, even though he was most likely innocent of the charges.

- In 1559 Elizabeth I issued a proclamation forbidding any contemporary references to events or persons in the theater. The reason was to avoid making "greatness familiar" (Greenblatt, 2004, p. 339).

- The Union Jack flag design was proposed by James I as a symbolic uniting of the kingdoms of England and Scotland. The red Saint George's cross over a white background and the white Saint Andrew's diagonal cross over a blue background were overlaid to represent a united nation to the world.

- Bear baiting, when a bear is chained to a stake and attacked by dogs, was so popular in 17th-century England that Elizabeth I would treat foreign ambassadors to this "sport."

- In J. K. Rowling's *Harry Potter and the Chamber of Secrets* (1998) Dumbledore's phoenix is named Fawkes after the notorious Guy Fawkes from the Gunpowder Plot in 1605.

Resources

The following contains a sampling of resources for a study of *Macbeth* in the classroom. Below you will find available DVDs, operas, books and stories, and a listing of Web sites. In addition, educators may be interested in the extensive secondary sources referenced in the "Suggested Readings" list to supplement a teaching of the play.

DVD

Preview all DVDs to ensure that the scenes are appropriate for your community. Sometimes a scene or two will make the point. Another option is to assign a DVD to watch at home.

- *Macbeth* (1979) directed by Trevor Nunn: Starring Ian McKellen and Judi Dench, the minimalist adaptation brilliantly captures the descent of the Macbeths. Shot originally in 1979, this relatively newly released DVD (2004) is an acting tour-de-force. Particularly noteworthy is the unenthusiastic, exhausted "Hail! King of Scotland" from a bloody Macduff addressing Malcolm.

- *Scotland, PA* (2001) directed by Billy Morrissette: A clever take on *Macbeth*, Morrisette sets the play in small town Scotland, PA, where Macbeth and his wife work at a luncheonette aptly named Duncan's. Instead of blood on her hands, Lady Macbeth burns her hand from the grease in a fryer.

- *Macbeth* (1997) directed by Jeremy Freeston: This very teachable version of the play stars Jason Connery, Sean Connery's son, playing the role of Macbeth. Although there are a number of familiar faces in this production, you will not recognize the names of the actors. This detail, however, does not matter, because the production is very well done.

- *Macbeth* (1971) directed by Roman Polanski: This bloody production also features a naked coven of witches, a naked Lady Macbeth sleepwalking, and a naked Macduff's son taking a bath. The nudity in all the examples is brief. Some teenagers will enjoy the bloody Macbeth-Macduff battle at the end.

- *Throne of Blood* (1957) directed by Akira Kurosawa: Kurosawa retells the story and sets it in feudal Japan. A brave warrior is pushed by his wife to kill the emperor. The foggy atmosphere of the forest establishes an effective mood for betrayal. Although subtitled, this high-quality film portrays character well.

❧ *Macbeth* (1948) directed by Orson Welles: Orson Welles of *Citizen Kane* fame acts in and directs this black-and-white version of *Macbeth*. Although it may be interesting to see the young Welles at the beginning of a fine acting and directorial career, this film version is very slow for school-aged students who are studying the play. The film does work well when comparing and contrasting it with other versions of the play.

Opera

❧ Verdi's *Macbeth* (1972): The Washington National Opera performs Verdi's first Shakespearean opera. A portion of an audio version of the performance may be accessed at http://www.npr.org/templates/story/story.php?storyId=14058055. Verdi uses 18 witches instead of three. They are singing opera, after all.

❧ Shostakovich's *Lady Macbeth of Mtsensk* (1936): Disgusted by "the score's modernism," Stalin walked out of the 1936 opera, which is centered on Katerina, a bored housewife who takes a lover. Adultery and murder soon follow (Heyworth). Copies of this opera can be bought on Amazon.com.

Books and Stories

❧ *A Charmed Life: Growing up in Macbeth's Castle* (2008) by Liza Campbell

❧ *Bullets for Macbeth* (1976) by Marvin Kaye

❧ *Lady Macbeth: A Novel* (2009) by Susan Fraser King

❧ *Macbeth the King* (1981) by Nigel Tranter

❧ "The Macbeth Murder Mystery" (1943) by James Thurber

❧ *Macbird!* (1967) by Barbara Garson

❧ *The Third Witch* (2002) by Rebecca Reisert

❧ *Wyrd Sisters* (2001) by Terry Pratchett

Informative Web Sites

Background: Holinshed's *Chronicles* (1587): http://www.clicknotes.com/macbeth/Holinshed

Royal Shakespeare Company: http://www.rsc.org.uk/exploringshakespeare/teachers/forteachersmacbeth.htm

Bloody Tyrant or Benevolent King: Will the Real Macbeth Please Stand Up? http://www.sff.net/people/catherine-wells/Shakesp.htm

Web English Teacher: *Macbeth*: http://www.webenglishteacher.com/macbeth.html

Enjoying *Macbeth*: http://www.pathguy.com/macbeth.htm

The Land of *Macbeth*: http://www.thelandofmacbeth.com/macbeth.htm

Mr. William Shakespeare and the Internet: http://shakespeare.palomar.edu

Shakespeare Resource Center: *Macbeth*: http://www.bardweb.net/plays/macbeth.html

Macbeth: Commentary and Analysis: http://www.shakespeare-online.com/playanalysis/macbeth.html

Macbeth: A Study Guide: http://www.cummingsstudyguides.net/xMacbeth.html

Globe Theater: Virtual Tour: http://www.shakespeares-globe.org/virtualtour/stage

Suggested Readings

Adelman, J. (1991). *Suffocating mothers: Fantasies of maternal origin in Shakespeare's plays*—Hamlet *to* The Tempest. New York: Routledge.

Blair, D. (1996). What happens in *Macbeth* Act I, Scene VII? *The Review of English Studies, 47,* 534–539.

Bloom, H. (1998). *William Shakespeare's* Macbeth: *Bloom's reviews*. Broomall, PA: Chelsea House.

Bloom, H. (1999). *Shakespeare: The invention of the human*. New York: Riverhead.

Boswell-Stone, W. G. (1968). *Shakespeare's Holinshed: The* Chronicles *and the plays compared*. New York: Dover.

Breuer, H. (1976). Disintegration of time in Macbeth's soliloquy "Tomorrow, and tomorrow, and tomorrow." *Modern Language Review, 71,* 256–271.

Chamberlain, S. (2005). Fantasizing infanticide: Lady Macbeth and the murdering mother in early modern England. *College Literature, 32*(3), 72–91.

Coursen, H. R. (1997). Macbeth: *A guide to the play*. Westport, CT: Greenwood Press.

Delaney, B. (2001). Shakespeare's *Macbeth. Explicator, 60,* 7–9.

Delaney, B. (2004). Shakespeare's *Macbeth*. *Explicator, 63,* 6–9.

Delaney, B. (2005). Shakespeare's *Macbeth*. *Explicator, 63,* 209–211.

Gallagher, K. (2003). *Reading reasons: Motivational mini-lessons for middle and high school*. Portland, ME: Stenhouse.

Gardner, H. (1993). *Multiple intelligences: The theory in practice*. New York: Basic Books.

Guj, L. (1986). *Macbeth* and the seeds of time. *Shakespeare Studies, 18,* 175–188.

Horwich, R. (1978). Integrity in *Macbeth*: The search for the "single state of man." *Shakespeare Quarterly, 29,* 365–373.

Jensen, E. (2001). *Arts with the brain in mind*. Alexandria, VA: Association for Supervision and Curriculum Development.

Kállay, G. (2003). Was Macbeth lying? The "be-all," the "end-all," and the ethics of time. *European Journal of English Studies, 7,* 137–149.

Legatt, A. (2005). *Shakespeare's tragedies: Violation and identity*. Cambridge, England: Cambridge University Press.

Mackie, J. D. (1984). *A history of Scotland*. New York: Penguin. (Original work published 1964)

Shapiro, J. (2006). *A year in the life of William Shakespeare: 1599*. New York: HarperPerennial.

Silver, H. F., Strong, R. W., & Perini, M. J. (2000). *So each may learn: Integrating learning styles and multiple intelligences*. Alexandria, VA: Association for Supervision and Curriculum Development.

Strunk, W., Jr., & White, E. B. (2008). *The elements of style* (50th Anv. ed.). New York: Longman.

Swisher, C. (Ed.). (1999). *Readings on* Macbeth: *The Greenhaven Press literary companion to British literature*. San Diego, CA: Greenhaven Press.

Tufts, C. (1998). Shakespeare's conception of moral order in *Macbeth*. *Renascence: Essays on Values in Literature, 50,* 169–182.

References

Aitchison, N. (1999). *Macbeth: Man and myth*. Phoenix Mill, England: Sutton.

Barnet, S. (1956). Coleridge on Shakespeare's villains. *Shakespeare Quarterly, 7,* 9–20.

Baer, W. (2006) *Writing metrical poetry: Contemporary lessons for mastering traditional forms*. Columbus, OH: Writer's Digest Books.

Beecher, J. (1988). *Note-taking: What do we know about the benefits?* (ERIC Digest, 12). Bloomington, IN: ERIC Clearinghouse on Reading and Communication Skills. (ERIC Document Reproduction Service No. ED300805)

Billmeyer, R., & Barton, M. L. (2002). *Teaching reading in the content areas: If not me, then who?* (2nd ed.). Alexandria, VA: Association for Supervision and Curriculum Development.

Brooke, N. (1990). Introduction. In N. Brooke (Ed.), *The tragedy of* Macbeth (pp. 1–81). New York: Oxford University Press.

Campbell, L. (1968). *Shakespeare's tragic heroes*. New York: Barnes and Noble.

Faires, R. (2000, October 13). *The curse of the play*. Retrieved June 7, 2008, from http://www.austinchronicle.com/gyrobase/Issue/story?oid=oid:78882

Fraser, A. (1996). *Faith and treason: The story of the Gunpowder Plot*. New York: Nan A. Talese/Doubleday.

Garber, M. (2008). *Shakespeare and modern culture*. New York: Pantheon Books.

Gaskill, M. (2005). *Witchfinders: A seventeenth-century English tragedy*. Cambridge, MA: Harvard University Press.

Godshalk, W. (1965). Livy's Tullia: A classical prototype of Lady Macbeth. *Shakespeare Quarterly, 16,* 240–241.

Greenblatt, S. (2004). *Will in the world.* New York: Norton.

Harcourt, J. (1961). "I pray you, remember the Porter." *Shakespeare Quarterly, 12,* 393–402.

Harris, N. (2000). *Heritage of Scotland: A cultural history of Scotland and its people.* London: Checkmark Books.

Henneberger, O. (1946). Banquo, loyal subject. *College English, 8*(1), 18–22.

Hosley, R. (Ed.). (1968). *Shakespeare's Holinshed: An edition of Holinshed's* Chronicles *(1587).* New York: Capricorn Books.

Hummell, L. (2006). Synectics for creative thinking in technology education. *Technology Teacher, 66*(3), 22–27. (ERIC Document Reproduction Service No. EJ747942)

Jehl, D. (1999, January 31). Uneasy lies the prince who gets a letter from the king. *The New York Times,* Section 4, p. 7.

Jolliffe, D. A. (2001). *AP language and composition seminar.* Lecture presented at DePaul University, Chicago.

Jonson, B. (1989). To the memory of my beloved master, the author, Mr. William Shakespeare, and what he hath left us. In M. H. Abrams & S. Greenblatt (Eds.), *The Norton Anthology of English Literature* (7th ed., pp. 648–650). New York: Norton. (Original work published 1623)

Mangan, M. (1991). *A preface to Shakespeare's tragedies.* Essex, England: Longman.

Marzano, R. J., Pickering, D. J., & Pollock, J. E. (2001). *Classroom instruction that works: Research-based strategies for increasing student achievement.* Alexandria, VA: Association for Supervision and Curriculum Development.

Mehl, D. (1983). *Shakespeare's tragedies: An introduction.* Cambridge, England: Cambridge University Press.

Moncur, M. (2007). *Patriotism quotations.* Retrieved May 15, 2008, from http://www.quotationspage.com/subjects/patriotism

Mowat, B. A., & Werstine, P. (Eds.). (2004). *Macbeth.* New York: Washington Square Press and Folger Shakespeare Library.

Muir, K. (Ed.). (1992). *Macbeth* (10th ed.). Liverpool, England: Arden Shakespeare.

Nolan, R. (1913). The law of the seal of confession. In C. G. Herbermann, E. A. Pace, C. B. Pallen, T. J. Shahan, & J. J. Wayne (Eds.), *The Catholic encyclopedia* (Vol. 13, p. 649). New York: Robert Appleton. (Original work published 1907)

Nostbakken, F. (1997). *Understanding* Macbeth: *A student casebook to issues, sources, and historical documents.* Westport, CT: Greenwood Press.

Oczkus, L., & International Reading Association. (2003). *Reciprocal teaching at work: Strategies for improving reading comprehension.* (ERIC Document Reproduction Service No. ED480245)

Padelford, F. (1901, April). Macbeth the thane and Macbeth the regicide. *Modern Language Notes, 16,* 112–119.

Paul, H. N. (1950). *The royal play of* Macbeth. New York: MacMillan.

Raphael, T., & Au, K. (2005). QAR: Enhancing comprehension and test taking across grades and content areas. *Reading Teacher, 59,* 206–221. (ERIC Document Reproduction Service No. EJ738005)

Rowse, A. L. (1963). *William Shakespeare: A biography.* New York: Harper and Rowe.

Saccio, P. (Speaker). (1999). Macbeth: *Fair is foul. Shakespeare: Comedies, histories, and tragedies.* (Compact Disc). Chantilly, VA: Teaching Co.

Santa, C. M. (1988). *Content reading including study systems: Reading, writing and studying across the curriculum.* Dubuque, IA, Kendall/Hunt.

Schoenbach, R., Greenleaf, C., Cziko, C., & Hurwitz, L. (1999). *Reading for understanding: A guide to improving reading in middle and high school classrooms.* San Francisco: Jossey-Bass.

Sharpe, J. (1999). *The bewitching of Anne Gunther: A horrible and true story of deception, witchcraft, murder, and the king of England.* New York: Routledge.

Snyder, A. D. (1923). A note on Coleridge's Shakespeare. In *Modern Language Notes, 38*(1). Retrieved May 13, 2008, from http://www.jstor.org/stable/2914784

Tomlinson, C. A. (2003). *Fulfilling the promise of the differentiated classroom: Strategies and tools for responsive teaching.* Alexandria, VA: Association for Supervision and Curriculum Development.

Tromly, F. (1975). Macbeth and his porter. *Shakespeare Quarterly, 26,* 151–156.

Vincent, T. (2008). *Podcasting.* Retrieved April 24, 2008, from http://learninghand.com/podcasting

Winstanley, L. (1970). Macbeth, King Lear, *and contemporary history.* New York: Octagon Books.

Wood, M. (2003). *Shakespeare.* New York: Basic Books.

Wormeli, R. (2005). *Summarization in any subject: 50 techniques to improve student learning.* Alexandria, VA: Association for Supervision and Curriculum Development.

Wylie, J. A. (1887). *History of the Scottish nation.* Retrieved August 1, 2008, from http://www.electricscotland.com/history/wylie/vol1ch12.htm

About the Authors

After 32 years, Daniel G. Lipowitz continues to teach seniors, juniors, and sophomores honors and academic English, Creative Writing, and Film as Art and Literature at Unionville High School in Kennett Square, PA. A graduate of Pennsylvania State University and the University of Pennsylvania, he has directed 35 plays, including the "Scottish Play." In addition, Lipowitz is the advisor of the award-winning school newspaper, *The Indian Post*. He also serves as an SAT essay grader. His hobbies include playing guitar, writing songs, and being player–manager of his men's softball team, the Tornadoes. He has produced and composed songs for a children's album, *Music for Little Humans*. Also, Lipowitz composed "A September Morning"—a song honoring the heroes of Flight 93. Lipowitz has created the "Monsters of Literature" podcasts, a series of interviews on the iTunes Store. An avid fan of the Philadelphia Phillies, he resides in Ardmore, PA, with his outstanding wife, Lorraine, and their spectacular children, Anna and Nathan.

James M. Conley teaches 11th- and 12th-grade honors and Advanced Placement English at Unionville High School in Kennett Square, PA. An alumnus of The College of the Holy Cross in Worcester, MA, and Villanova University in Villanova, PA, Conley currently is pursuing his doctorate in education at Widener University in Chester, PA. He is an adjunct English professor at a number of colleges in the Philadelphia region, namely, Saint Joseph's University, West Chester University, Cecil College, and Delaware County Community College. Conley works with secondary and postsecondary learners helping them to develop their analytical thinking skills and to discover their voice as a writer. The 2006–07 Unionville High School "Teacher of the Year" and the 2004–05 recipient of the "Teaching Excellence Award" from Saint Joseph's University, Conley enjoys reading, spending quality time with his family, and cheering on all Philadelphia sports teams, especially the Philadelphia Eagles. He resides in Oxford, PA, with his fabulous wife and best friend Michele and their two energetic and carefree sons Jimmy, Jr. and Joey.